Forms of Explanation

Forms of Explanation

RETHINKING THE QUESTIONS
IN SOCIAL THEORY

ALAN GARFINKEL

New Haven and London
Yale University Press

Published with assistance from the
Kingsley Trust Association Publication Fund
established by the Scroll and Key Society of Yale College.

Designed by Nancy Ovedovitz
and set in IBM Press Roman type.
Printed in the United States of America by
Vail-Ballou Press, Binghamton, N.Y.

Library of Congress Cataloging in Publication Data

Garfinkel, Alan, 1945–
  Forms of Explanation

  Includes index.
  1. Hermeneutics. 2. Reductionism. 3. Social sciences–Philosophy.
4. Relativity. 5. Philosophy. I. Title.
BD241.G36   300′.1   80–23341
ISBN 0–300–02136–4

1 2 3 4 5 6 7 8 9 10

To my parents

If social science is the answer, what is the question?

Contents

Preface

In the course of my education, and in the writing of this book, I have had the help of a large number of people.

Foremost acknowledgment goes to my parents, Sam and Paulyne Garfinkel, whose sacrifices made my education possible and whose support has been large and ever present.

Another but for whom is Hilary Putnam, who found me as a graduate student in a basket on his doorstep and gave me essential nurturance. His friendship and encouragement have been very important to me over the years. My intellectual debt to him will be obvious to those who know his work; it goes well beyond the explicit references in the text.

I was fortunate to have had some outstanding teachers at Cornell and at Harvard. Their support and that of my friends have been essential to my work. It is a pleasure to acknowledge the friendship of my friends, and the cheerful debts of endless conversations. Andrea Nye provided support and stimulation during a crucial period. I have also benefited from many conversations on these topics with Cheyney Ryan. Other friends, like Josh Cohen, also supplied valuable points. Naomi Scheman and others provided useful comments on an earlier draft, but whatever errors or inaccuracies remain are the fault of David Hills, who read an earlier draft at a heroic level of detail, and provided useful comments and pleasurable talks. Jane Isay furnished a wonderful mix of friendship, advice, and criticism.

I am very grateful to these people, and to many more.

Introduction

We are surrounded by explanations. The child is failing at school because he or she has a low IQ. Prices are going up because of inflation. Inflation exists because "too many dollars are chasing too few goods." We do not normally stop to ask what these explanations mean or what they are supposed to be explaining. This can lead to problems. Often we first become aware of trouble when we encounter conflicts, when several explanations, coming from different angles and speaking to different aspects of a problem, crowd around a single object. We look at a body of theory and find a confusing patchwork of schools and approaches, and it is very hard to see how they fit together.

This happens all the time in the social sciences. In psychology alone we find Freudians (of various kinds), behaviorists, cognitive developmentalists, physiological psychologists, holistic psychologists, humanistic psychologists, transactionalists, gestaltists, social psychologists, symbolic interactionists, personality theorists, existential psychoanalysts, and perception theorists, to name just the best-known varieties. Add this to similar lists for economics, sociology, anthropology, and linguistics, and we have a bewildering variety of ways of approach and modes of explanation.

Faced with any such list, what strikes us is the difficulty of finding a coherent way of comparing the different theories. They seem to be different *sorts* of things. Some of the theories may address different phenomena or different realms of phenomena. Some are genuinely competing, others can be reconciled with one another, while still others pass one another by, answering different questions. They fit together only in a very complicated and overlapping geometry.

It will help to try to map out this geometry. As theoreticians we need to understand how the explanations relate to one another, and as consumers of explanations, people who are trying to deal with some concrete problem, we need to understand how explanations answer or fail to answer the questions we are asking. What is needed is an analysis of explanation that will help us to sort out this variety. My aim here will not be to construct a general philosophy of explanation based on first principles. Instead I will look at a variety of examples and attempt by their means to develop some elements of a theory. The examples are chosen with an eye to the central questions a philosophy of explanation must deal with:

> When are two explanations inconsistent with each other?
> When are two explanations irrelevant to each other?
> When can two explanations from different theories be added or joined to each other?
> How does one explanation replace or supplant another?
> When does one explanation presuppose another?
> When are two explanations from different theories really explaining the same thing?
> What could make one explanation superior to another? /

Explanations in Conflict

If a child is failing at school, there are an embarrassingly large number of potential explanations. If the child happens to be black, there are even more. A short list of explanations includes: low IQ (genetic or environmental causes), culture of poverty, lack of proper prenatal diet, institutional racism, bad teachers, "cultural remnants of slavery," biased educational standards, lack of appropriate role models, economic pressures, matriarchal families, minimal brain damage, and lack of future orientation.

Now what do all these explanations have to do with one another? Are they competing? Do they reinforce one another? Are they complementary to one another, or perhaps just irrelevant to one another, existing on different levels? The person who thinks that the explanation lies in brain damage clearly disagrees with the person who thinks that it is a matter of biased teachers, and both reject an explanation in terms of matriarchal family structure. Yet it is far from clear how we know that these are mutually exclusive.

This is an example of the most basic problem in sorting out a mass of explanations: Which of them are in conflict with which others? As the example illustrates, this can be a very hard question to answer.

On occasion it is easy, if the inconsistency is right on the surface of the explanations themselves. "There was a conspiracy to kill John F.

Kennedy" is inconsistent with "Oswald acted alone." But usually the conflict is not obvious from the formal structure of the statements, and then our analysis of it depends a great deal on background theory and assumptions.

We hear discussions, for example, of conflicts between genetic and environmental explanations of race differences. Someone says that something is "eighty percent explained by genetics"; someone else says, "No, it is eighty percent environmental." They seem to agree that the form of explanation is that any trait is $x\%$ due to genes and $100 - x\%$ ("the rest") due to environment. But are genetic explanations really in conflict with environmental ones? Are they jointly exhaustive? The answer is *no*, in both cases, although this is not understood by many of the participants in these arguments.

At the very least it seems that before we plunge into such debates we should try to sketch what the basic categories of explanation are. This is not usually done, in part because of the sheer difficulty of deciding when two explanations are really in conflict.

Neither is it clear what to do when faced with apparently conflicting explanations. Must we opt for one or the other? Or is it somehow possible to maintain both?

In quantum mechanics the principle of complementarity says that for certain purposes an electron can be viewed as a particle, while for other purposes it can be viewed as a wave. The two modes of explanation, particle theory and wave theory, attribute inconsistent properties to the electron and therefore cannot be applied simultaneously. Yet neither one is true to the exclusion of the other. I am inclined to think that this duality is intolerable: future science will have to eliminate it in favor of a single, coherent picture. Others welcome it as a paradigm in physics itself of the possibility of multiple "conceptual frameworks" or "points of view." And anytime two rival forms of explanation seem applicable to the same thing, it can be tempting to see a case of complementarity. For example, mind and body can be viewed as providing complementary modes of explanation of human action (psychology and physiology). But is there any validity to this view beyond the superficial similarities? We do not know what is going on in the quantum mechanics case, and even less whether there are any genuine examples of complementarity on the macroscopic level.

So we see that among the members of a collection of explanations there will be a number of distinct kinds of relations, straightforward and

complicated. Of course, a multiplicity of explanations does not necessarily mean that there is any internal contradiction at all. Consider this set of explanations of the death of Socrates:
Socrates died because:

> Athens feared his independence
> he drank hemlock
> he was tried and convicted of a capital offense
> he suffered cardiac/respiratory arrest secondary to ingestion of coniine alkaloid
> he was too closely linked to the antidemocratic forces
> he refused Crito's offer of escape.

Here the explanations are not mutually contradictory. Some are different parts of the story, others treat the event on different levels or from the standpoint of different kinds of inquiry. All of them can be maintained simultaneously.

These examples suggest that the first task we might set for a philosophy of explanation is that it give us some account of these conflicts, complementarities, overlaps, and displacements, that it give, as it were, an elementary algebra of explanations. Its purpose would be to tell us when they can be added together and when they must be subtracted from one another.

Whatever Happened to Neurasthenia?

The variety is further complicated by the fact that there are not only different explanations but different conceptions of what an explanation *is*. Perhaps the most important intellectual development of the twentieth century has been the recognition that there is a variety of conceptual frameworks, forms of understanding, or cognitive points of view. Like a Cubist painting, the contemporary world-picture features a simultaneous presentation of multiple perspectives.

We no longer understand the development of science as a smooth, linear growth of a monolithic entity, Knowledge. Rather, we see it as marked by discontinuities in conceptualization, by radical shifts in the very idea of what the problem is and of what a scientific explanation might look like.

The source of this understanding can ultimately be traced back to Kant's demonstration that the forms of empirical knowledge are subject to prior categories of the understanding. Once we see how concepts shape our knowledge and perception, we see how other categories and other concepts could produce radically different forms of knowledge and explanation. For Kant, these categories were given once and for all; later came the realization that they are changing and developing, determined and conditioned by period, culture, and context. T. S. Eliot writes:

> Even Kant, devoting a lifetime to the pursuit of categories, fixed only those which he believed, rightly or wrongly, to be permanent, and overlooked or neglected the fact that these are only the more stable of a vast system of categories in perpetual change.[1]

Recent history and philosophy of science have stressed the idea that developments in knowledge often take the form, not of discoveries of new facts, but of shifts in the conception of what the phenomena to be explained are and of what counts as an explanation of them. The work of Bachelard on conceptions of fire and space, of Foucault on hospitals, madness, and prisons, and more recently the writings of such people as Toulmin and Kuhn have made people more aware of the ways in which the science of a particular period views the world through concepts very much its own.

Thus the prescientific view of the heavens was that everything revolved around man; the early scientific revolution inverted that to say that everything revolved aound the sun. But the modern view calls into question the very concept of something "revolving around" something else. Strictly speaking, nothing "revolves around" anything else.

Consider some of the ways in which psychology has characterized the objects of its explanations and the styles of explanation appropriate to those objects. We are inclined, for instance, to think of physiological explanation in psychology as something recent, but in fact it has been very much in vogue at other times as well. Seventeenth-century psychology postulated physiological explanations of behavior in terms of airs, humors, and other material substances. Sir Robert Burton's classic treatise *The Anatomy of Melancholy* discusses melancholy as a pervasive and general condition and sees it as a fundamental psychological diagnostic category. He says that people become melancholic when a certain material humor in them changes from sweet to sour, a process he likens to wine turning to vinegar. They become melancholy "as vinegar out of the purest wine . . . becomes sour and sharp." He goes on to show how this explanation also accounts for other observed

---

1. In his introduction to Charlotte Eliot's *Savonarola: A Dramatic Poem* (London: R. Cobden-Sanderson, 1926), p. viii.

phenomena of melancholy: "From the sharpness of this humour proceeds much waking, troublesome thoughts and dreams, etc."[2]

Now what *is* this? An explanation? An analogy? A metaphor? It is all
of these really. The distinctions are not hard and fast to begin with, and
some things can be substantive theories at one point and literary meta-
phors at another (e.g., "that makes my blood boil"). At least the *form*
of Burton's explanation is more or less familiar to us, although we have
some trouble understanding what exactly is the object being explained,
this condition called "melancholy." Nowadays we do not use this as a
general descriptive term, and so the object of explanation for us will be
different. Part of what "melancholy" meant would be covered by our
(that is, the current psychoanalytic) concept of "depression." But only
part of it. The rest corresponds to other current concepts or to no concept at all. The recent edition of Burton has a jacket description that
characterizes "melancholy" as "a term used in the seventeenth century
to cover everything from schizophrenia to a lover's moping." "Schizophrenia," on the other hand, is a twentieth-century term used to cover
everything from out-and-out madness to political dissent. It has been
severely criticized as ideological by Foucault, Szasz, Laing, and others.

Earlier in this century, melancholy would have been diagnosed as
"neurasthenia," a term then very much in fashion among psychologists.
In fact it was one of their main diagnostic categories and was applied
to everything from depression to shyness and anemia. It is no longer
used at all, and it was formally dropped as a diagnostic category by the
American Psychological Association some years ago. The epic account
of the conquest of neurasthenia waits to be written.

Radical changes in styles and objects of explanation can be found in
all the sciences, not just psychology. When Galileo reported seeing moons
circling Jupiter, he was refuted by a priori arguments that there could
be no such thing, since the number of planets (i.e., objects in the solar
system) was necessarily seven. The explanation of why there had to be
seven took the form of correlating them with the seven apertures of
the human head!

> There are seven windows given to animals in the domicile of the head,
> through which the air is admitted to the tabernacle of the body, to en-
> lighten, to warm and to nourish it. What are the parts of the *micro-
> cosmos*? Two nostrils, two eyes, two ears and a mouth. So in the heav-
> ens, as in a *macrocosmos*, there are two favorable stars, two unpropi-

2. *The Anatomy of Melancholy* (1621) (New York, Vintage Books, 1977), p.
174.

tious, two luminaries, and Mercury undecided and indifferent. From
this and many other similarities in nature, such as the seven metals, etc.,
which it were tedious to enumerate, we gather that the number of planets is necessarily seven.[3]

This case is different from Burton's psychology, which we can vaguely
assimilate to our own modes of explanation. First of all, the style of explanation, the microcosm–macrocosm analogy, is one that we cannot
assimilate to any model we currently use. But there is more. The "fact"
which is being explained, the existence of seven planets, is of course
no fact at all. There are not seven, there are nine, or more, depending
on what you count. But the real problem lies in the very idea that this
is the kind of thing that can be explained at all.

After all, suppose there are nine planets. *Why* is this so? What explanation does modern astrophysics give us for the fact? It turns out that
there is no nontrivial explanation. Modern science rejects the idea of explaining that sort of thing, except by the trivial statement that that is
how many there turned out to be. Here the difference is not about facts
but about what kinds of facts we can expect to explain.

We can distinguish two different issues. The first concerns changes in
the general form of the explanation, while the second concerns changes
in the object of explanation. In the first case we see claims that one
form of explanation is to be rejected in favor of another, while in the
second there are shifts and dislocations in the very nature of the phenomena being explained or even in what is held to be capable of explanation
at all. We need a term to refer to these modes of explanation and associated objects; I propose to call them *explanatory frames*. An explanatory frame is therefore a model or paradigm of a form of explanation
and an object to be explained. 错位 混乱

Answers and Questions
Perhaps the most interesting cases of changes in explanatory frames are
ones in which there is a shift in the nature of the *question* being asked.
Explanations are sometimes answers to explicit questions. Why is the sky
blue? Why do metals expand when heated?[4] But often there is no

3. From Charles Taylor's *Hegel*, p. 4. Taylor is quoting from S. Warhaft, ed.,
Francis Bacon: A selection of his works (Toronto, 1965), p. 17.
4. For one treatment of explanations as answers to questions, see S. Bromberger,
"Why Questions," in B. Brody, ed., *Readings in the Philosophy of Science* (Engle-
wood Cliffs, N.J.: Prentice-Hall, 1970), and "An Approach to Explanation," in R.
J. Butler, ed., *Studies in Analytical Philosophy*, 2nd ser. (Oxford: Blackwell, 1965).

explicit question at hand, and in those cases it can be very instructive to perform a kind of diagnostic inference and ask what question the explanation is really answering.

The emphasis on questions, and on ferreting out the implicit question behind an explanation, is crucial to this entire work. Attending to the questions rather than the answers and looking for the implicit question hiding behind the answer are a useful device for analyzing explanations and understanding historical shifts. In general, epochs in history, the history of science or any other history, are marked as much by the questions they ask as by the answers that they give.[5]

The first example I want to examine, from physics, concerns the shift from medieval to Newtonian theories of motion.[6] The medieval physicists looked at an object in motion and asked, Why does it keep moving? This seemed like a natural question, and there had to be some answer to it, some kind of force that keeps the object moving. They called it "impetus".

Newton rejected such forces. But he did not offer in their place an alternative explanation for why the object keeps moving. Instead, the "explanation" he did offer was peculiar: he said that things do not need anything to keep moving, and hence that the question was mistaken. An object in motion just tends to remain in motion unless acted on by an outside force. In a certain way, this is trivial. Not as a scientific advance, for it was a major scientific breakthrough, but trivial as an answer to the question "Why does the object keep moving?" For it says, in effect, "It just keeps moving." Newton rejected this question and by doing so rejected the forces that the medievals had postulated. Even though those forces were, in the current phrase, "inferences to the best explanation," the explanatory frame that required them was rejected.

The shift to the Newtonian explanatory frame is a shift to thinking that what stands in need of explanation is not why an object is moving but rather why the motion of an object *changes*. What stands in need of explanation is acceleration, change of motion, not motion itself.

Toulmin describes this by saying that when the body is in constant

5. Marx writes (in the *Grundrisse,* trans. M. Nicolaus [New York: Random House, 1973]): "Frequently the only possible answer is a critique of the question, and the only solution is to negate the question."

6. The facts of my account are drawn from the discussion in Toulmin's *Foresight and Understanding,* the chapter entitled "Ideals of Natural Order" (New York: Harper & Row, 1961).

motion, the "body's motion is treated as self-explanatory."[7] The statement that the motion is self-explanatory and the statement that it is explained only trivially amount to the same thing, that the explanation takes the form of saying that something happened because nothing prevented it from happening. By themselves, such explanations tell us nothing. It does not help us to be told that Saturn has rings because nothing happened to prevent it from having rings.

The role of such vacuous explanations is not to stand on their own as independent, informative statements, but rather to signal us that we have reached the outline of the explanatory frame we are using. It tells us what sorts of things we try to explain, and in what ways. If an airplane crashes, we ask why and expect an answer. But suppose flight 123 is a normal, routine flight and arrives safely. If we ask, Why didn't flight 123 crash?, there is no answer except: because nothing happened to make it crash. What we are saying is that we do not explain safe flights the way we explain crashes.

The second example of a shift in explanatory frame is one from evolutionary biology. Aristotle wondered why we have the species that we do. That is, if we look at the species that exist, they are an odd lot. There are, for example, porcupines and giraffes but no unicorns. Why are there no unicorns? The set of actually existing species forms a haphazard subset of the set of all possible species. It becomes natural, in a certain frame of mind, to ask why this or that species was or was not actualized. Why these and not those?

Aristotle wanted a genuine answer to this. He rejected as unscientific the view that species are generated randomly ("by chance") and then either survive or do not. If a particular species exists, there has to be some nontrivial answer to the question of why it exists. This leads him to the conclusion that "it is plain then that nature is a cause, a cause that operates for a purpose."[8]

We are inclined to think Aristotle naive, or prescientific, and to feel self-congratulatory about the "the modern theory of evolution," but we should first ask what answer modern biology *does* give to Aristotle's question. Why *are* there no unicorns? It turns out that there is no real answer given, at least no nontrivial one. Mutation and natural selection does not tell us why there are no unicorns; it just says that there happen

7. Ibid., p. 55.
8. *Physics* 199 b 32.

never to have been any. This is different from the case of dinosaurs, in which there *is* a nontrivial answer to the question of why they do not exist: the environment could not support them, or something like that. It is also different from the question of why there are no flying horses, for there is also a real answer to that: flying horses are mechanically impossible. But with unicorns there is no such answer.

Darwinian biology simply does not answer Aristotle's question. The scientific advance that Darwin made can partly be seen as a rejection of that question and the substitution of a different question, namely: *given* that a species comes to exist (however it does), why does it continue to exist or cease to exist? That is precisely not the question of the origin of species but rather why species survive. This question *is* given a nontrivial answer. And so, once again, the shift from one explanatory frame to another consists of a shift in the question.

Questions and Purposes

The examples given above should illustrate the importance of a sense of the question in understanding historical developments. Such a sense is also important for understanding explanations here and now, for they exhibit a similar kind of relativity. The variety of potential questions that can be asked produces a relativity of possible explanations. This can give rise to misunderstandings, cases where it *looks* like people are disagreeing about the correct explanation of something but where they are really answering different questions.

A couple was once discussing in my presence the reasons for the breakdown of their relationship. Various factors were offered as the explanation, and fairly soon it became obvious that there were a number of different questions that were being argued at cross purposes. The last straw for the couple had been a fight they had had after one of them was involved in an auto accident. There was mention of the accident itself as the cause of the crisis, but people have accidents all the time without causing breakups in their relationships. Therefore, we must distinguish the question

What brought on the crisis? (the auto accident)

from the question

What caused it to precipitate a crisis?

This is only the beginning. Other questions must be distinguished, the answer to each of which could claim to be "the" explanation of the breakup:

> Why did the fight over the accident lead to the breakup of the couple?
> Who started the fight?
> Whose fault is the general situation?
> What could change it now?
> What should these people learn for the future from this?

The answer to every one of these questions can, in one context or another, be called the explanation of the breakup.

As we begin to realize the multiplicity of questions that can be asked, it is natural to wonder how we could ever choose among them. Looking at this example, we can begin to see certain themes. The most basic differences among the questions are the differences in their practical point of view: they are oriented toward different purposes. For example, the answer to the first question, What brought it on?, may be "the auto accident." But it may be *pointless* to dwell on this fact; there may be no purpose served by that question, no future in it. Things like that happen, we would say; the question is, Why did it have that effect? Here the shift in question is being urged for a practical reason.

Sometimes there are whole classes of questions which are practically useless in the way that dwelling on the auto accident can be useless. Certain ways of questioning may focus on the wrong aspects of the situation or be the wrong questions to ask. This is one way in which value considerations enter into the choice of explanation (see chaps. 5 and 6 below). One explanation may be better than another because it lends itself to practical use better than the other.

Perhaps the simplest kind of case is the one where the requirement is simply that the explanation *be* pragmatic. We sometimes reject a particular form of explanation because it gives us no practical handle on the situation. This is the position that B. F. Skinner takes toward Freudian explanation in terms of an "unconscious." His claim is not that there is no such thing as the unconscious but rather that explanations in terms of it are *useless*: "The objection to inner states is not that they do not exist, but that they are not relevant in a functional analysis."[9] The criteria for what goes into a "functional analysis" are basically practical.

9. *Science and Human Behavior* (New York: Macmillan, 1953), p. 35.

Therefore he dismisses explanation in terms of inner mental states (as well as explanations in terms of physiological states of the nervous system) as "of limited usefulness in the prediction and control of specific behavior" (p. 29). This, in turn, is true because any explanatory factor is "useless in the *control* of behavior unless we can manipulate it" (p. 34).

This is a quite particular view of the relation between explanation and practical control, in a sense the most extreme view. There are several faults with it. First of all, the relation between practical control and goodness of explanation is not as straightforward as Skinner has it. The Copernican, heliocentric view of the solar system does not give us manipulable factors or practical control any more than the Ptolemaic system does. Explanations in geology—say, of the formation of continents — do not give us the ability to predict or control, but they are good explanations for all that.

The second fault with Skinner's extreme pragmatism is that it is not at all clear that explanations in terms of the unconscious really do fail his practicality test. Such explanations *are* of practical help, at least sometimes. Classical psychoanalytic explanations *sometimes* help people change their behavior, and so it is simply a mistake to dismiss them on the grounds that they have no practical or therapeutic consequences.[10]

Questions and Objects

The example of the couple breaking up teaches a basic lesson: We need to pay more attention to what exactly is being explained by a given explanation. Too often, theories *talk* as if they are addressing some problem, though they are really addressing different problems or different aspects, interpretations, or readings of the problem. For when a theory talks about a phenomenon, it inevitably does so in terms of its own representation of it. The phenomenon gets incorporated into the theory in a particular way, structured by a definite set of assumptions and presuppositions about its nature. This makes it very important that we recognize those presuppositions and discover how the theory has represented a particular object of explanation.

---

10. It is a very interesting question to ask *how* this is so. How exactly does the psychoanalytic explanation of my behavior enable me to change it? How does finding out, for example, that something I am doing is "really" an expression of hostility toward my father help me to change what I am doing?

Recall, for example, the explanations of racial patterns in education. Notice that some of them are addressing a sociological phenomenon, others a phenomenon of individual psychology. Which of these is right? Is the phenomenon individual or is it sociological? How are these aspects related? These questions have to be faced before we can consider any particular theory because they are asking what *kind* of problem is being addressed. Any given theory would have to, as a precondition, address the "right" interpretation of the question, on pain of irrelevance (or worse). at the risk of

Or consider theories of "aggression." Sociobiological theories talk of genetically programmed territorial aggression. There are instinct psychologies that speak of aggressive drives and Freudian theories that treat aggression as a defense against imagined castration. How many phenomena have we just named? Do we have here three competing explanations, or explanations of three different phenomena?

The work that needs to be done here is *pretheoretical*. We have to bring to the situation some understanding of what the phenomena are that we want explained. There are two distinct problems: first, to decide when two theories are talking about the same thing, and second, to decide whether a theory is really speaking to the problem we intuitively want answered. We must find a way of describing these pretheoretical phenomena and construct, somehow, the common ground on which their explanations meet. This means making the connection between the pretheoretical understanding of the problem and the ways in which various theories turn that understanding into a definite problematic.

Very often, a theory will substitute a technical formulation for an intuitively conceived problem. When this happens, it may be difficult to say to what extent this theoretical, technical formulation captures the "real" problem.[11] This substitution may take place quickly and silently, unacknowledged by the theoretician and unnoticed by the questioner. If the substitution is not faithful to the problem, the questioner may be in the position of asking for bread and being handed a stone. Joan Robinson remarked that this is characteristic of economics.

We might, for example, be concerned about schools and the problems

11. Goethe wrote, in *Maximen und Reflexionen,* "Mathematicians are like Frenchmen: whatever you say to them they translate into their own language and forthwith it is something completely different" (cited by Morris W. Hirsch, *Differential Topology* [New York, Springer-Verlag, 1976], p. 169).

people are having in them. We might be led to think about this as the problem of why some people "do well" in school and other people "do poorly." We might then be led to think about it as a problem of "intelligence." A bit later we would find ourselves in the middle of a discussion of IQ, talking about what factors influence it and what its distribution in the population is. From there it is a short step to talking about IQ rank correlations when controlled for SES, and to ask how "predictive" or how "heritable" they are.

The relation of any of these technical formulations to the original problems is far from clear. It is time to start reexamining the technical concepts of the social sciences to see what their presuppositions are. There is an ultimate sense in which the definition of the problem must be in pretechnical, *human*, terms. The spread of science, especially social science, has effected a revolution in which the influence of human concerns no longer shows itself in the shape of the theory. In a way it is a kind of Copernican revolution: a decentering of human concerns relative to the scientific scheme of things. But there is a sense in which the Copernican revolution was mistaken: people *are* the center of the universe, at least in the sense that ultimately human concerns shape physical theory. Physical theory ultimately revolves around us, even if the planets do not.

The sense of this has been largely lost in recent theorizing in the social sciences. It is very hard to recognize the objects of our concern in the technical terms of modern social science. It is time for a humanist counterrevolution, reasserting the primacy of our pretheoretical, ethical, concerns. What is needed is a critical philosophy of explanation. Its point would be to give us an understanding of what the objects of explanations are, what we want them to be, what forms of explanation are appropriate to those objects, and how various explanations fit together, excluding or requiring one another, supplanting one another historically, presupposing one another.

Reductionism
One of the deepest relations that one explanation can have toward another is that of *reducibility*. The reductionist claims that one class of phenomena, more or less well explained by some body of theory, is really explainable by some other theory, which is thought of as deeper or more basic. This, we might say, reduces the apparent complexity of the world.

Some of the most basic claims of science are to be found in examples of reduction. Is all human behavior reducible to the working out of unconscious sexuality? This is a simple example of a reduction. So is the claim to explain all human behavior in terms of stimulus conditioning. Many social theorists (I think wrongly) cite Marx as the source for their view that all social phenomena are reducible to economics. Regardless of who held it, it is an important reduction to understand. Other reductions, also influential, have been based on biology and seek to explain social phenomena as the working out of various biological imperatives. Examples of this range from the social Darwinist and Malthusian social theories of the 1800s to the contemporary discussion about biologically based "aggression" or "territoriality" or the recent sociobiology.

The pull of reductionist views is very strong. They give us a kind of understanding that we regard as profound. When Newton demonstrated that terrestrial phenomena, like falling bodies, and celestial phenomena, like planetary motions, could be brought under a *single* set of laws, the effect on the general world view was profound. For before Newton, no two things could be more different than leaden weights falling from earthly towers and the patterns of the heavens. Newton changed this. The same sort of conceptual power, the ability to change the way we see a large class of phenomena, makes reductions very attractive, be they physical, biological, economic, sexual, or any other kind.

In this work I examine reductionism from the point of view of the theory of explanation. Does the reducing theory in these various examples really give us *explanations* of the phenomena? In order to answer this, we will have to look more closely at the explanations that are being offered, but we shall also have to examine the notion of explanation itself. What exactly is it that we are looking for when we seek these kinds of reductive explanations?

One answer is that we are looking to go beyond the ordinary explanations we give of phenomena. The power of Marxist or Freudian or sociobiological explanations is precisely that they give us a radically *new* view of what is "really" going on in what we thought was a familiar realm. The ordinary phenomenon is displayed transformed by the reductionist explanation. This fact, which gives power to reductionist explanations, is also responsible for the most basic problem: Are the new phenomena explained by the reducing theory really the same phenomena as the familiar ones? The reducing or underlying theory is supposed to explain the same phenomena as the reduced or upper-level theory. This presupposes that one explanation is an explanation *of the same phenomenon* as the other.

But is the "aggression" that sociobiology seeks to explain the same aggression we find in war or civil strife? Is it the same aggression that Freud talked about? Is the "social stratification" of the recent IQ theorists the same stratification that economics and sociology try to explain? Is it the same as the stratification Marx speaks of?

Sometimes, as we shall see, the answer is no, and when it is, a simple-minded reductionism will be untenable. But the surprising thing is not that the answer is sometimes negative but that this essential question is usually not even asked. Writers on this subject make claims which turn on such questions, yet they use the notions of explanation and its objects in an unreflective and uncritical way.

The question of when two explanations are explanations of the same phenomenon is another of the basic problems in sketching our algebra of explanations. It is fundamental for understanding such earlier questions as when two explanations are inconsistent with each other and when one explanation supplants another. Since reduction involves the notion of explanation across theories, the problem of the identity of the objects of explanation is crucial here.

Individualism

In one of the most basic forms of reduction a theory of one realm of phenomena is reduced to an underlying theory whose objects are the physical constituents of the objects of the first theory. Such a reduction tries to explain the phenomena of one "level" by appeal to the theory of what the things on that level are made of. Following standard practice, we shall call such reductions *microreductions*.

The paradigm of microreduction in physical science is the reduction of thermodynamics, the theory of the observable properties of gases (temperature, pressure, and so forth), to statistical mechanics, which postulates that the gas is made up of certain kinds of molecules. One then derives the higher-level laws from the lower-level mechanical assumptions. This is often taken as a paradigm of microreduction, not just in physical science, but in social theory as well.[12] In general its strategy is

12. *Social theory* is the term I am using indiscriminately to refer to social science, social philosophy, and their various mixtures. Obviously, the use of this term suggests that I do not think that a "normative vs. positive" distinction can be usefully drawn. In fact, all the examples partake of the nature of both.

to explain the upper-level phenomena by showing how they arise from the interaction of the atomic constituents.[13] This is an extremely powerful form of explanation and has had an enormous influence.

When this paradigm is applied in social theory, we get the various forms of *individualism*. What they all have in common is the idea that the characteristics of society can be explained as arising from the characteristics of individuals, just as the characteristics of the gas can be explained as arising from the properties of its molecules. What the specific theory of the individuals is, of course, varies from case to case. It may be the psychoanalytic theory of individual psychology, as in Freud's *Civilization and Its Discontents,* or it may be a biological theory of the formation of individual characteristics, as in the recent sociobiology. It may be the commonsense explanation-by-reasons of the actions of individuals, as in traditional narrative history, or again it may be the explanation of individual choices of the kind represented by rational-choice theory in economics.

The essence of these is the methodological form of explaining social phenomena from individual phenomena. This is the guiding methodology of much contemporary social theory, the subject of much debate; under the name *methodological individualism,* it has been discussed both by philosophers and by social scientists. Clear endorsements of methodological individualism can be found in Hobbes, Locke, Adam Smith, Mill, and Weber among the classics, and in contemporary social scientists like Kenneth Arrow and George Homans.[14] In contemporary social theory, it is the guiding methodology of such work as:

> Theories of the market that seek to explain economic phenomena as arising from the sum of individual choices (Milton Friedman, F. A. Hayek)
>
> The work of social-choice theorists in attempting to reduce the problem of collective choice to the theory of individual choice (K. Arrow, Mancur Olson, A. K. Sen)
>
> Attempts to reduce the problem of distributive justice to the justification of individual "holdings" (Nozick)

13. There are, therefore, cases of microreduction that are not atomistic, for example, a microreduction where the underlying level is a continuous medium. Such cases will not concern us here.

14. Nozick's *Anarchy, State and Utopia* (New York: Basic Books, 1974) contains a useful list of sixteen examples of individualist explanations (p. 20).

Theories of political representation which seek to construct an overall political decision out of the individual preferences (Buchanan
and Tullock, Downs)

The methodological issue has been the subject of much debate; yet,
for all that, the debate is of little help in understanding the controversy.
Partly, this is because the debate is muddled by an astonishing variation
in the theses called "methodological individualism." We have, for example: theses about what kinds of entities are "real" (or "really real"),
theses about how we *know* about social phenomena, theses about the
"derivability" of certain kinds of laws from others, and theses about
what kinds of explanations exist or are "ultimate" ones. Writers use
these variants interchangeably and will often shift from one to another
in the course of an argument.[15]

This lack of clarity is especially alarming because if there is one thing
that everyone agrees on, it is that the debate is of more than academic
interest and that important moral and political issues are lurking in the
background. Karl Popper's *The Open Society and Its Enemies* is a two-
volume blast at all nonindividualistic social theory. He says that failure to
grasp methodological individualism leads not only to philosophical and
scientific error but to moral and political evil. Plato, Hegel, and most of
all Marx are the examples he cites of what can happen if we are not individualistic; the consequences are totalitarianism. Nonindividualists, he
suggests, believe in trampling, in thought and deed, on individual liberty.
On the other hand, other writers have pointed out that individualism
is itself not without ideological consequences and presuppositions.

The main focus of this work is the assessment of individualism, both
as a general philosophy of social explanation and as a guiding methodology. I join the controversy because I think it is a chance for philosophy to be useful in the analysis of real scientific and social issues. The
principal strategy will be to attack the problem via an examination of
the concept of explanation itself. Methodological individualism, like all
species of reductionism, consists in a claim that certain kinds of explanation are available, that the theory of individuals explains the phenomena
which were previously the province of the upper-level social theory.

15. Lukes's survey article "Methodological Individualism Reconsidered," in A.
Ryan, ed., *The Philosophy of Social Explanation* (Oxford: Oxford University
Press, 1973), distinguishes *eight* importantly different theses, including some, but
not all, of the above!

Is this true? Do the individualistic explanations really explain the same things as their holistic counterparts? I argue that the answer is often no. In particular I argue in the second half of this work that certain kinds of individualistic explanations are "bad" ones, while other kinds of "structural" explanations are "good" ones.

Wanted: A Philosophy of Explanation

The task, then, is to gain a clearer view of the phenomena of explanation, the shifts and dislocations in explanatory frames, and the other characteristic relations among explanations and their objects. We need an account of the algebra of explanations. Such an account would have theoretical interest but, what is more, could be of real use to the consumer of explanations in sorting out the Babel evidenced in the first pages of this chapter. It could function as a kind of consumers' guide to the explanatory marketplace.

What follows falls short of such a general philosophy of explanation. Only scattered and partial answers are given to the questions raised. I will make some remarks in the direction of those questions and try to sort out some kinds of explanations from some others. I will suggest that, in certain cases, some explanations are preferable to others. I will also be claiming that some explanations are really answering different questions than they might appear to be.

The reason I have not trimmed this introduction to fit the modesty of what follows is that I think a general philosophy of explanation is really needed and it is valuable to set out the questions that have to be answered. It is something of a scandal how little attention has been paid to this need by traditional philosophy, which, with just a few exceptions, has had virtually nothing to say about the forms of explanation.[16] This is not just an oversight. The philosophy of science, for the first half of this century, was dominated by logical positivism, an approach that featured a single formal model for all explanation; all explanation was seen as formal deduction of sentences from general laws.[17] Any explanation

16. There has been some attention paid to the subject outside traditional academic philosophy. See Hayden White, *Metahistory: The Historical Imagination in Nineteenth-Century Europe* (Baltimore: Johns Hopkins University Press, 1973), and Stephen C. Pepper, *World Hypotheses* (Berkeley and Los Angeles: University of California Press, 1966).

17. The "deductive-nomological" model of Hempel's *Aspects of Scientific Explanation* (New York: Free Press, 1965).

that did not conform to this model was either defective or "not really scientific."

This is not the place for a critique of this doctrine. I will have more to say about it in chapter 5. It is not my goal to offer a detailed criticism of the positivist model. Rather, I want to move beyond it, to take a position in post-positivist philosophy of explanation, via a consideration of the kinds of questions I have posed in this introduction. The formal, positivist, model gives us either no answers at all to those questions or answers that are just false.

1 Explanatory Relativity

When Willie Sutton was in prison, a priest who was trying to reform him asked him why he robbed banks. "Well," Sutton replied, "that's where the money is."

There has been a failure to connect here, a failure of fit. Sutton and the priest are passing each other by. The problem is to say *how,* exactly, they differ. Clearly there are different values and purposes shaping the question and answer. They take different things to be *problematic* or stand in need of explanation. For the priest, what stands in need of explanation is the decision to rob at all. He does not really care what. But for Sutton, that is the whole question. What is problematic is the choice of what to rob.

We could say that Sutton and the priest have different notions of what the relevant alternatives to bank robbing are. For the priest, the relevant alternative to bank robbing is leading an honest life, not robbing anything. But for Sutton, the relevant alternatives to bank robbing are: robbing grocery stores, robbing gas stations, and so on. What Sutton is really explaining is why he robs banks *rather than* robbing grocery stores, etc. We could say that the priest has asked why Sutton *robs* banks and Sutton has answered why he robs *banks!*

The difference between them is that they have two different *contrasts* in mind, two different sets of alternatives to the problematic: Sutton robs banks. They are embedding the phenomenon to be explained in two different spaces of alternatives, which produces two different things-to-be-explained, two different objects of explanation.

The object of explanation here is therefore not a simple object, like an event or a state of affairs, but more like a state of affairs together with a definite *space of alternatives* to it. In the Sutton case the priest's object is

Sutton $\left\{ \begin{array}{l} \text{does not rob} \\ \text{robs} \end{array} \right\}$ banks, whereas Sutton's object is

$$\text{Sutton robs} \begin{Bmatrix} \text{other things} \\ \text{banks} \end{Bmatrix}.$$

Clearly, if the same event is embedded in two different contrast spaces, the answers to the two different questions so generated will not necessarily be the same, and will often be different. Many jokes, like the Sutton joke, have as their structure a question and answer having different presuppositions, and often this will take the form of a dislocation from one contrast space to another. Children's jokes make use of this device in such classics as: Why do firemen wear red suspenders? (To keep their pants up); and: Why do ducks fly south in the winter? (It's too far to walk). Sometimes, as with Sutton, the answerer answers a question that is much narrower in scope than the intended question. Sometimes it is the reverse, as the answerer answers a very general interpretation of a narrow question. The detective, questioning a suspect about a murder, asks the suspect, Why did he die? The suspect tentatively suggests, Well, everyone has to go sometime, sir. Here, the suspect is dodging the detective's "real" question. The explanation is formally an answer to the question, but what is really being answered is the very general question why

$$\text{the victim} \begin{Bmatrix} \text{lived forever} \\ \text{died} \end{Bmatrix},$$

whereas the detective's question was really why

$$\text{the victim} \begin{Bmatrix} \text{died at some other time} \\ \text{died} \end{Bmatrix}.$$

The effect of such differing spaces of alternatives is not always a joke; what aspect of a given state of affairs we take to be problematic radically affects the success or failure of potential explanations. For an explanation to be successful, it must speak to the question at hand, whether explicit or implicit, or else we will have failures of fit like Sutton and the priest. What we need, therefore, is some way of representing what is really getting explained in a given explanation, and what is not. The contrast spaces give us such a representation of one basic way in which explanation is "context relative." My claim is that this relativity-to-a-contrast-space is quite general; I will call it *explanatory relativity*.

Once sensitized to this phenomenon, one can easily find examples of it, for there are many cases in which explanations are rejected as belonging to the "wrong" contrast space. For example, at one point in his analysis of dreams, Jung is discussing a dream about an auto accident:

> We reduce the dream-picture to its antecedents with the help of the dreamer's recollections. He recognizes the street as one down which he had walked on the previous day. . . . The car accident reminds him of an accident that had actually occurred a few days before, but of which he had only read in a newspaper. As we know, most people are satisfied with a reduction of this kind. "Aha," they say, "that's why I had this dream."
> Obviously this reduction is quite unsatisfying from the scientific point of view. The dreamer had walked down many streets the previous day; why was this one selected? He had read about several accidents; why did he select this one?[1]

The complaint is that a certain contrast is crucial for a successful explanation, and that some would-be explanation fails to account for that contrast. A good example is furnished by Meyer Shapiro's "Nature of Abstract Art,"[2] which considers and rejects the standard forms of explanation for the rise and fall of artistic styles: explanations that appeal to "the exhaustion of possibilities" in earlier styles and "pendulum swing" theories. His complaint is: "From the mechanical theories of exhaustion, boredom and reaction we could never explain why the reaction occurred when it did" (p. 190). Later he criticizes one such explanation for the rise of Futurism, saying that it "makes no effort to explain why this art should emerge in Italy rather than elsewhere" (p. 208).

On a more abstract level, Aristotle complains that atomists try to explain movement by postulating an eternal motion of the atoms. But, he says, this is a poor explanation because it does not explain why things move one way rather than another.[3] And, at the other extreme, explanations in everyday life also reflect this relativity, as advertising slogans urge: "Don't ask me why I smoke. Ask me why I smoke Winstons."

1. C. G. Jung, *The Structure and Dynamics of the Psyche* (Princeton: Princeton University Press, 1966), p. 240.
2. Meyer Shapiro, "Nature of Abstract Art," in *Modern Art: 19th and 20th Centuries* (New York: George Braziller, 1978).
3. "Why and what this movement is they do not say, nor, if the world moves one way rather than another, do they tell us the cause of its doing so" (*Metaphysics* 1071 b 33).

Yet despite the frequent occurrence of explanatory relativity, not much attention has been paid to the general phenomenon. There are several good examples in a recent paper by Fred Dretske. Here is one of them:

> Suppose Alex, after being fired, needs some money to meet expenses until he finds another job. Clyde lends him $300. It seems fairly obvious that there are three different questions (at least) that we can ask with the words "Why did Clyde lend him $300?" and, accordingly, three different explanations one can give for Clyde's lending him $300. We may want to know why Clyde lent him $300. The answer might be that this is how much Alex thought he would need; or perhaps, though Alex wanted more, this is all the ready cash that Clyde had available. On the other hand, we may want to know why Clyde *lent* him $300—why didn't he just give it to him? . . . Finally, we may be interested in finding out why *Clyde* lent him $300.[4]

Here, the three different explanations can be represented as the answers to the questions:

1 Why Clyde lent Alex $\left\{ \begin{array}{l} \$300 \\ \text{some other} \\ \text{sum} \end{array} \right\}$

2 Why Clyde $\left\{ \begin{array}{l} \text{gave} \\ \text{lent} \end{array} \right\}$ Alex $300 and

3 Why $\left\{ \begin{array}{l} \text{someone else} \\ \text{Clyde} \end{array} \right\}$ lent Alex $300.

Dretske observes that the differences among various stresses is essentially of a *pragmatic* nature and says that examples like these "constitute serious obstacles to any attempt to formulate a purely syntactical characterization of explanation."

This is true. But then how *should* we characterize it? Dretske represents the variations by using contrastive stress, the linguists' term for the device of underlining (or vocally stressing) part of the sentence. But the voice or the underline is a symptom of whatever is going on here, not an analysis of it. And in addition to not being an analysis, it cannot represent the more general forms of explanatory relativity, since it is obviously

4. Fred Dretske, "Contrastive Statements," *Philosophical Review* 82 (Oct. 1973): 419.

limited to cases where the problematic consists of a variation in one of the explicit syntactic parts of the sentence. If the aspect being varied is not a syntactic part of the sentence, contrastive stress cannot represent the explanatory relativity. For example, take the case of Clyde lending Alex $300, and suppose that we know that Alex is the sort who, if he could not raise the money from friends, would take Willie Sutton's advice and rob a bank. Clyde knows this too and so lends his friend $300 to keep him from getting into trouble.

If we then asked, "Why did Clyde lend Alex $300?" and received the answer: to keep his friend out of jail, how are we to represent the "real" question? It is not:

1. why *Clyde* (rather than Bob) lent Alex $300

or 2. why Clyde *lent* (rather than gave) Alex $300

or 3. why Clyde lent *Alex* (rather than Phil) $300

or 4. why Clyde lent Alex *$300* (rather than some other sum)

but rather why Clyde lent Alex $300 (without emphasis) *rather than* letting him rob a bank. The contrast space is the only possible representation in cases like these.

The Algebra of Explanations

Let us begin, then, with the simple idea that an explanation always takes place relative to a background space of alternatives. Then different spaces of alternatives may therefore require different explanations. And sometimes we can compare two explanations to see how their contrast spaces differ. This gives us a measure of the dislocation between two explanations.

Contrast spaces therefore give us a useful tool for comparing explanations with each other. In particular I want to go back to the examples of the introduction and show how sometimes a shift from one explanatory frame to another is just a shift in the relevant contrast space. Consider the case of Newton vs. the medieval physicists: The medievals asked why something keeps moving. Their object can now be represented as asking why

$$\text{the thing is} \left\{ \begin{array}{l} \text{moving} \\ \text{not moving} \end{array} \right\} \text{at } t,$$

In order to answer this, they had to postulate a force acting at each time.

We are now in a position to represent the epistemological break that Newton achieved.[5] It is to reconstitute the object of explanation as asking why

$$\text{the thing has} \begin{cases} \text{given acceleration} \\ \text{some other acceleration} \end{cases} \text{at } t.$$

For this object the only nontrivial explanations are explanations of changes of motion, that is, of accelerations. So the break from the medievals to Newton can be represented as a shift in the contrast space of their explanations.

The same things can be said about the other example of that section, the shift from Aristotelian to evolutionary biology. Aristotle asked why there are the species that there are. We can now state the object of his question: he was asking why these species exist *rather than* the other possible species, that is, why

$$\begin{cases} \text{other possible species} \\ \text{these species} \end{cases} \text{exist.}$$

The shift to the Darwinian question is the shift to explaining *not* the origin of species but rather their survival. In other words the object becomes why

$$\text{these species} \begin{cases} \text{become extinct} \\ \text{exist} \end{cases}.$$

This representation makes a little clearer what is and what is not getting explained in a given explanation. And this, in turn, means that the problems of explanation discussed in the introduction are sensitive to the contrast space phenomenon.

Consider, for example, the problem of deciding if pretheoretical questions are really being answered. Certainly a necessary condition for a theory to be a real answer to a pretheoretical question is that it embody

---

5. The terminology ("coupure epistemologique") is taken from Bachelard. We could also have said "change in explanatory frame," or for that metter, "paradigm shift," "scientific revolution," "change in episteme" or "aspect shift." There are embarrassingly many terms, all of vague meaning, and all meaning vaguely similar things. I choose Bachelard's term because it greatly predates the others. See G. Bachelard, *The Psychoanalysis of Fire* (Boston: Beacon Press, 1964), and *The Poetics of Space* (New York: Orion Press, 1964).

a contrast space compatible with that of the question. Otherwise, failures to communicate like the one involving Sutton and the priest will occur. This happens more often than we realize and we will see more examples of it.

It is not just a matter of *what* in the explanation is being varied, it is also a matter of *how much*. Even though two questions agree on what in the original state of affairs is problematic, they may differ importantly on how large a space of alternatives they envision. If the question is why Clyde (rather than Bill) lent Alex $300, this may require a different answer than if the question is why Clyde (rather than Bill or Fred or Sue) lent Alex $300.

These expansions and contractions in the space of imagined alternatives occur fundamentally and often, and they play a strong role in shaping what counts as an explanation. Suppose, for example, that we are discussing the 1968 presidential election and we ask why Nixon won the Republican nomination. A political historian tells us, Because all the other viable candidates had offended some segment of the party: Goldwater, Rockefeller, and Romney all had enemies within the party, and only Nixon had no one very strongly opposed to him. In this explanation the contrast space is

$$\left\{ \begin{array}{l} \text{Goldwater} \\ \text{Romney} \\ \text{Rockefeller} \\ \text{Nixon} \end{array} \right\} \text{won the Republican nomination.}$$

These are the live possibilities, and the explanation really does explain why Nixon won as against this contrast space. But the explanation would not work if we were entertaining some other possibility as live, say, that of Senator Percy getting the nomination. If we did, the political historian would have to add something like: The delegates to the convention were well-entrenched conservatives for whom Senator Percy was too liberal.

Explanatory relativity is also relevant to the other problems of the introduction; the algebra of explanations is greatly affected by variations in the contrast space. Two explanations are inconsistent with each other, or can be conjoined, or are irrelevant to each other, only if their contrast spaces line up in certain ways. If one explanation presupposes another, its contrast space will be a refinement or partition of one of the elements of the contrast space of the other (as in the Sutton case). In each case there is more to be said about how contrast spaces enable us to represent these relations, and about how the various relations among explanations correlate with various relations among their contrast spaces.

In particular this is true of the problems of theoretical reduction. We said that one of the main requirements of a would-be reduction is that it enable us to explain "the same phenomena" as the prereduction theory. But this notion of "the same phenomena" is clearly sensitive to explanatory relativity: two different contrast spaces may smuggle in a Suttonesque ambiguity into the situation. Consequently, in evaluating all reductionist claims, we must be careful that the objects match up and that the reducing theory really does explain the same phenomena (with the same contrast space) as the reduced theory. This will be one of the main tools I will use in the next chapter, in the analysis of reductionism.

Presuppositions of Explanations

The general claim of explanatory relativity is the claim that explanation takes place relative to a contrast space. I mean this as a claim about how to explain explanations: the contrast space is a basic presupposition of the explanation context, an additional piece of structure necessary to explain how explanations function.

Without some such hypothesis, I do not think we can give an account of how explanations actually work, or fail to. The contrast space determines, in part, what counts as a successful explanation. I want to examine this more closely, especially the idea of what really does get explained, and what does not, in a typical explanation. For there is an important way in which certain things really do not get explained. Now of course any explanation leaves *something* unexplained, and in particular any part of the object of explanation that is outside the contrast space will not be explained.

But there is something more. Look at the explanation that Sutton gave. The question was: why do you rob banks? and the answer was: they have the most money. He is saying, in other words, that the fact that

something has the most money

explains why

Sutton robs that thing.

Now we might, especially if we were sympathetic to the priest, ask *why* the first thing explains the second thing. Why, after all, does the fact that something has the most money explain why Sutton robs it? Note that it follows from the form of his explanation that, since it is (in some sense) necessary that something (or other) has the most money, there-fore, necessarily, Sutton robs something. The fact that Sutton robs some-thing or other follows from the form of the explanation.

But this is just the thing that is bothering the priest. He wants to know why rob anything at all, a question Sutton has not answered. But it is not just that he has not answered it. Rather, Sutton's answer *and the fact that it is taken to be an answer* (i.e., an explanation) indicate that Sutton is *presupposing* a satisfactory answer to the priest's question. He is presupposing it in the simple sense that his answer does not even make sense unless one supposes the priest's question already to have been ans-wered satisfactorily. Someone for whom the priest's question still lingers is not someone who can accept that Sutton's answer is an answer at all, for the implicit question which Sutton is answering is

> Given that you are going to rob something, why do you rob banks?

So the underlined phrase is a presupposition in the straightforward sense that whether or not one accepts it affects the success of the explana-tory act.

Looking at how such "given" clauses function in explanations gives us another view of the phenomenon of explanatory relativity. The "given" clause often (but not always) functions to express the same presupposi-tion as the contrast space. Roughly speaking, the question

> *Given* A, why B?   Van Frassen

is equivalent to the contrast

> Why B *rather than* any of the other alternatives to B in which A
> is true?

The "given" clause tells us, at the very least, what the outer bound is on the variation in B: we are to consider only such alternatives to B as also sat-isfy A. Why must this be so? Why is it that explanations limit their alter-natives in this way? Why do we have explanations of why X rather than Y, or why A, given B, rather than simply explaining why X or why A?[6]

6. Notice, incidentally, that this very question has the form "Why P rather than Q?"

The answer, I think, lies in our need to have a *limited* negation, a determinate sense of what will count as the consequent's "not" happening. Lacking such a determinate sense of alternatives, one has difficulty seeing how we could give explanations at all; they would have to be so all encompassing as to be impossible.

Let me give an example. Suppose that I got up one day and went out for a drive. I was doing about 110 when I rounded a bend, around which a truck had stalled. Unable to stop in time, I crashed into the truck. Later, chastising me for the accident, you say, "If you hadn't been speeding, you wouldn't have had that accident." I reply, "Yes, that's true, but then if I hadn't had breakfast, I would have gotten to that spot before the truck stalled, so if I hadn't eaten breakfast, I wouldn't have had the accident. Why don't you blame me for having had breakfast?"

What's wrong with my reply? It is based on the truth of a causal conditional: if I had not had breakfast, I would not have had that accident. But while it is true that I would not have had *that* accident, nevertheless, if I had been speeding then it is likely that I would have had *another* accident. My claim is based on the assertion that if something (eating breakfast) had not happened, the accident would not have happened. The problem is, What is going to count as that accident's not happening? If "that accident" means, as it must if my statement is going to be true, "that very accident," that concrete particular, then *everything* about the situation is going to be necessary for it: the shirt I was wearing, the kind of truck I hit, and so forth, since if any one of them had not occurred, it would not have been *that* accident.

But this is absurd, and in order to escape this absurdity and not have everything be necessary for the accident, we must recognize that the real object of explanation is not

my having had that accident.

We need something in addition to represent what is really getting explained, something that will account for the fact that my objection somehow misses the point. For not *any* difference from that very accident is going to count as relevantly different, only certain ones will. And so we need, in addition to the event, a set of perturbations which will count as irrelevant or inessentially different. These irrelevant perturbations determine an equivalence relation, "differs inessentially from," and the real object of explanation is an equivalence class under this relation.[7] The equivalence relation determines what is going to count as the event's not happening.

If we consider the auto accident we can see that, for the usual purposes, many "alternatives" will be considered as "not essentially different" under this equivalence relation. Having had a similar accident in a similar place driving a similar car but wearing a different colored shirt, for example, will count as "not essentially different." The equivalence relation determines the object of explanation in the sense that the explanation which we seek must not dwell on the factors which select *among* equivalent states of affairs but only on factors which are responsible for the accident's happening rather than some *in*equivalent state of affairs.

Of course, the exact specification of this equivalence relation, the specification of what exactly is going to count as relevantly different, is not given in advance or once and for all. The relation can be drawn tightly or loosely. In the auto accident case I am trying to evade responsibility by drawing the relation very tightly, thus making a great deal necessary for it to have occurred. I *am* prepared to say that an accident in which I was wearing a different shirt counts as "the same," and so I would not try to use the shirt as a necessary cause; I have *some* nontrivial conception of what counts as "the same" accident. But I have chosen (implicitly) a specific object of explanation. My detractors, blaming me for the accident, are insisting on a different equivalence relation. For them, the question is why I had that accident rather than not having had any accident. In other words they count my having had another accident just down the road as something which is essentially the same as what actually happened.

So each equivalence relation lays a grid or mesh over the possible phenomena, and corresponding to each mesh there is a conception of what the object of explanation is. We can, as in the auto accident, insist on one mesh or another. But the choice is not entirely arbitrary. There is a general fact which must be taken into account. As the mesh becomes finer and finer, that is, as the equivalence classes become smaller and more numerous, the resulting object, and hence the resulting explanation, becomes less and less *stable*. That is, the explanation:

7. Each equivalence class consists of the set of "inessentially different" objects, collapsed into one for this purpose.

reckless driving causes accidents (somewhere or other)

is highly stable under all sorts of perturbations of the underlying situation: the weather, road conditions, etc. We can perturb them almost at will, and the causal relation remains. On the other hand the explanation

reckless driving and breakfast and . . . causes accident at x, t, . . .

is highly unstable under these same perturbations. This is sometimes obscured by the fact that we call auto crashes "accidents." Sometimes a crash is really accidental, that is, is highly unstable with respect to its antecedents. But other times, as in this case, accidents are not accidental at all, even though we can (perversely) cast the object of explanation so as to make it seem accidental.

The general need to have an object of explanation which is somewhat stable under such perturbations means that the choice of object is not entirely arbitrary. Each equivalence relation determines the kind of object, and hence a theory, in much the same way as Felix Klein defined a geometry as arising when we specify an equivalence relation. Any equivalence relation, or sense of what is essentially the same as what, gives us a new set of objects. We study the features which are invariant under the various perturbations. Each equivalence relation therefore gives rise to a different "geometry." But which geometry is the "right" one? Clearly, there are some pragmatic, practical factors at work. Yet the situation is not completely determined by these factors, for these practical demands must be reconciled with the nature of the phenomena themselves and with the stability demands of good scientific explanation.

So the answer to the question, Are irrelevance-geometries stipulated, or are they "in the world"? is: both! We can stipulate equivalences at will, but the result will be a good explanation or a good piece of science only if the way *we* are treating things as inessentially different corresponds to the way *nature* treats things as inessentially different.

                    .   .   .

Let us grant, then, that when we explain an event not everything about it is essential to it. The explanation has to be stable in some neighborhood of the actual world. The problem now is: How large a neighborhood? What are its boundaries?

Clearly, the particulars of a specific explanation can be perturbed substantially while the explanation retains its force. If the explanation for why a leaf is green is that it contains chlorophyll, then the causal form:

contains chlorophyll   causes   green color

holds generally in a wide class of circumstances. But not in all circumstances: *jars* which contain chlorophyll are not caused thereby to be green. So obviously, there is a presupposition working here, to the effect that this case is the *kind* of case for which "contains chlorophyll" explains "greenness."[8] Again, if you sought to explain why something moved as it did by citing Newton's laws of falling bodies, you are presupposing that the thing in question is the kind of thing for which those laws hold, namely, a physical object, etc. If it turns out that the moving thing was a shadow on the side of a building, you must withdraw or amend your explanation, for we have passed out of the realm for which such explanations hold.

Each time, there is a presupposition that this case lies inside the domain of validity of the explanatory form, that is, that it is the *kind* of thing for which such an explanation can hold. Now this gives us a kind of test for the presuppositions of an explanation: see how large a neighborhood of the actual situation will maintain the validity of the explanation. The outer boundaries of that neighborhood will represent the presuppositions of the explanation. In the simple cases above, those presuppositions are, respectively, that we are dealing with a *plant,* and that we are dealing with a *physical object.*

The presuppositions become much more complex when we pass to more difficult cases. Recall, for example, the explanation of why Nixon got the Republican nomination: all the other major candidates had alienated some faction or other in the party. Certainly this is only an explanation if we are presupposing that the four major candidates were the only possibilities; but something more is true. Suppose someone said, "Well, I understand that the other candidates had offended sections of the party. But Nixon is so awful; why did they nominate anyone at

8. Alternatively, it could be suggested that the problem turns on the ambiguity of the word "contains." If plants contained chlorophyll like jars do, they would not necessarily be green. But this is really no different from what I am saying, which can be put as the presupposition that we are talking about "contains" in the sense appropriate to plants, what the word "contains" means in the category of plants.

all? Why not just pass? Or why didn't they compromise by nominating
the set of the four of them to run junta-style?"

Such possibilities are essentially beyond the frame of the explanation
given. In our language the form of the explanation was something
like: *given* that exactly one person receives the Republican nomination, why was it Nixon rather than Goldwater, and so forth? Once we
wander outside the boundaries of the given clause, the explanation
collapses. The domain of validity of this explanation includes only those
situations in which exactly one person receives the Republican nomination.

The same sort of thing is true of the Sutton case. Since the form of
his explanation

> X has the most money   explains   Sutton robs X,

it is clear that this explanation is valid only in situations in which Sutton
robs exactly one (kind of) thing. The fact that Sutton robs exactly one
thing, therefore, is true of every possibility envisaged by the presupposition. It is a pure consequence of the presupposition and is therefore not
itself explained. The same thing is true of the Republican nomination
case, in which the fact that the Republicans nominate exactly one person
is a pure consequence of the presupposition.

So every explanation must have *some* generality, yet it obviously cannot have complete generality. Somewhere in the middle, then, are the
boundaries of the realm for which the explanation holds. This will vary
from case to case, and in each case the size and shape of the outer boundary of contemplated possibility will reflect (part of) the presuppositions
of that explanation.

.   .   .

I will return immediately to these points, develop them further, and
then apply them to ferret out the presuppositions of various explanations. First, I want to take a brief detour and make essentially the same
points again, from a slightly different standpoint: a consideration of the
role of *laws* in explanations.

Many philosophers think that laws play an essential role in explanations. In fact the covering-law model of Hempel and Oppenheim says,
basically, that an explanation consists in subsuming the situation to be
explained under a law. The role of such laws in explanations is twofold.
First, the law is supposed to provide the necessary *generality* that an

explanation must have: to say that A causes B, Hume noted, is to say that A and B are instances of some more general relation. Second, the law is supposed to capture the idea of a *connection* between A and B, the causal connection whose existence means that A and B are not merely accidentally co-occurring.

Now, I do not want to get into the issue of whether the kinds of laws contemplated in the standard treatments really do capture these notions, or whether explanations really must contain laws in them at all. (Some people think not: Scriven, Arronson, and Davidson, for example, think that there must *be* a law but that the explanation need not *cite* it.)

All I want to do immediately is to follow the standard way of talking about "deductive-nomological" explanations and to restate some of the conclusions of the last few pages in that language. Let us start with a simple example. When I explain why the plant is green by saying that it contains chlorophyll, the law in this case is that all plants which contain chlorophyll are green. So far, so good. Now consider the example of the Republican nomination, which Nixon won by not alienating anyone. Is the law here something like

Anyone who does not alienate anyone gets the Republican nomination?

There are several problems with this. First of all, it clearly applies only to leading candidates. So we must add the qualification:

Anyone who   (1) is a leading candidate
and   (2) does not alienate anyone
        gets the Republican nomination.

But this still will not do. Suppose *two* people had not alienated anyone? What would have happened then? Here the law gives a confused answer. On the one hand there is nothing in either of the conditions, or their conjunction, to rule out the possibility of two people satisfying them jointly. On the other hand it is a logical consequence of the law that it can be true of exactly one person.

Let me take the second point first. "Gets the Republican nomination" can be expressed more explicitly as

becomes the one and only person who gets the Republican nomination.

It is a logical consequence of the law that exactly one person gets the nomination. This we have already seen. That exactly one person get the nomination is in some sense a necessary truth. Here this fact is expressed by the fact that it is a pure consequence of the law.

Why could not two people have the property of being leading candidates who had not alienated anyone? It was perfectly possible; it just did not happen to be. So the correct form of the law is therefore:

> *If* there happens to be a unique person among the leading candidates who has not alienated anyone, then that person becomes the nominee.

And so we see that if there had been two such people, the whole explanation would have to be withdrawn because the very applicability of the law depends on the condition that there is only one such person. It must be withdrawn completely in the case where two people have the necessary properties, and we must go out to look for a whole different form of explanation in the case where that happens.

The case is somewhat different in the Willie Sutton example, where the law is something like:

> *If* something has the (most) money, *then* Sutton will rob it.

What if several things had the most money? Several things *cannot* have the most money; it is part of the meaning of the word *most* that exactly one thing has the most money.[9] In this case the fact that there is exactly one thing satisfying the requisite properties is a necessary truth, not an additional assumption about what just happened to be.

And so it does not really matter for the time being whether we speak of presuppositions of explanations, pure consequences of the law, or consequences of the meaning of the terms being used, for in any case the conclusion is that in cases like these the fact that there is a unique thing satisfying a certain property is not explained but, on the contrary, is a necessary truth in one way or another.

So much for the role of laws in explanations. I ventured into it in order to show, using concepts which are philosophically familiar, how presuppositions function to shape the space of contemplated alternatives, the phenomenon I am calling "explanatory relativity."

9. Roughly speaking, and ignoring the possibility of ties.

Explanatory Relativity and the Philosophy of Explanation

Although, as we saw, there is no shortage of *examples* of explanatory relativity, there has not been very much discussion of it as a phenomenon in the philosophy of explanation. There are hints of it here and there.

Aristotle devotes the last section of book Z of the *Metaphysics* to a discussion of explanation. Book Z is concerned with expounding the nature of *substance,* the foundation concept of his metaphysics, and in the last section he says that we can "make another start" on that subject by considering the notion of *explanation* (*aitia*), "for substance is a kind of principle and explanation." He continues immediately:

> Now to ask why is always why
> something belongs to something else (1041 a 12).

He goes on to provide a number of remarks about what various questions really mean. In each case the real meaning of the question is given by what amounts to a contrast. He says generally that to ask why is to ask "why something of something else"; he criticizes questions of the form Why A? and says that a true question has the form Why does A belong to X?

> "Why does it thunder?" means "why is a
> noise produced in the clouds?"

In each case he gives, like this one, the first element is the variable or problematic factor, and the second element is the unchanging substance. So we are asking *of* this substance, X, why it is A. We can add: that is, why it[10] is A rather than not-A.

In adding this explicit contrast I am only filling in what Aristotle has said elsewhere: that substance terms do not admit contraries but that the attributes of substance do. Thus his dictum "Substance is that which bears contraries" means that the substance X can be A or not-A; the person can be musical or unmusical. The substance term itself, X, does not have a contrary. The general picture this gives us of explanation is that explanation is *of* some substance X and explains why X is A rather than not-A.

This brings Aristotle's formula into conformity with what I have been

---

10. And it is essential that what *it* is is *an X.*

saying. The "substance" term X expresses the presupposition, that which is (taken as) fixed. The variation "A rather than not-A" expresses the *limited* set of alternatives. I say "limited" because the alternatives to the state of affairs

A belongs to X

are those in which

not-A belongs to X.

But these do not exhaust all of logical space because they share a common presupposition, X.

This general schema captures the ordinary cases of explanations. When we ask why the sky is blue, Aristotle would say we are really asking of the sky why it is blue rather than some other color. In contrast space language, we are asking why

the sky is $\left\{ \begin{array}{l} \text{another color} \\ \text{blue} \end{array} \right\}$.

This means, first of all, that the existence of the sky itself is not problematic for this explanation, and second, that what *is* problematic is (only) the *color* of the sky.

The two terms of the explanation, the substance term and the variation term, are also related in a very important, and very Aristotelian, way: the substance term tells us what the form of the explanation is going to be. It will be whatever the appropriate form of explanation is for things of that category.[11] Consider the variable predicate "red," something which can be had or not had by various kinds of substances.

If we ask:

Why is X red?

even if we understand that to mean:

Why is X $\left\{ \begin{array}{l} \text{another color} \\ \text{red} \end{array} \right\}$?

we still do not have a determinate form of explanation until we know

11. More accurately, the substance term tells us which forms of explanation will be appropriate for which predicates. There is not just one kind of explanation for each kind of substance but several. The form of explanation of the color of the sky, for example, is different from the form for explaining why it is cloudy.

what *kind* of thing X is. There is not, in this view, one all-purpose form of explanation for why any old thing is red, be it a book or a person or a sky or a dream-image. Instead, there is one kind of explanation for each kind of thing that is red.

If we ask why a *person* is red, for example, the answer might be "from exertion" or "because of anger." But "anger" does not generally produce redness, only in *people*. Horses who are angry do not become red. Likewise if we ask why a piece of metal is red, the answer might be "because it was heated to a high temperature." But the general relation between being heated and becoming red is only a relation in the category of *metals*. If a fluid is heated, it does not become red.

In each case, then, when we ask why X is A, we get the answer that it is because it is B. But, in general, B-ness will explain A-ness only for the kind of thing that X is. The kind of thing that X represents is therefore a presupposition, in the sense of the previous section.

.   .   .

Outside the classical period[12] there has not been much discussion of the forms of explanation until fairly recently, although there are some remarks in scattered places which talk about the need for contrasts of various kinds. For example, Wittgenstein speaks in the *Tractatus* about "logical spaces" whose structure is exactly that of a contrast space:

> Each thing is, as it were, in a space of possible states of affairs. . . . A spatial object must be situated in infinite space. . . . A speck in the visual field, though it need not be red, must have some color; it is, so to speak, surrounded by color-space. Notes must have *some* pitch, objects of the sense of touch *some* degree of hardness, and so on.[13]

But remarks like these are not, and they were not intended to be, part of a philosophy of explanation, and the role of such contrast spaces in explanation has not received much notice.

One interesting exception is Josiah Royce. His seminars were often devoted to the concept of explanation, with various people presenting papers on very modern-sounding topics in "comparative methodology."

---

12. Cf. also Plato's discussion of the forms of explanation in the *Phaedo,* 97–107.

13. *Tractatus Logico-Philosophicus* (London: Kegan Paul, 1921), 2.013f.

(For example, the graduate student T. S. Eliot presented one on the relation between interpretation and explanation in comparative religion.) Florence Webster presented a paper on the notion of cause in biology. She argued for a notion which was "interestingly analogous to Mill's method of difference. It is, namely, that while you cannot find the cause for an event, you can find the cause for the difference between two events" (p. 133). The following interchange took place:

> Costello: What is interest?
> Miss Webster: Depends on choice of events you compare an event with.
> Royce: Interest is objective in being determined by environment. You compare with certain other events..
> Miss Webster: Depends on the context of the interesting objects.[14]

These contrast spaces are still not well understood objects. Their structure is not readily identifiable with any of the traditional objects of logic, for example. They have some similarities with "possible worlds," for instance, but they are not simply spaces of possible worlds. They are more like equivalence classes of possible worlds (under the relation "differs inessentially from") with almost all possible worlds excluded altogether from the space. (Contrast spaces are typically quite small.)

The basic structure of a contrast space is something like this: If Q is some state of affairs, a contrast space for Q is a set of states $[Qa]$ such that:

1. Q is one of the Qa.
2. Every Qa is incompatible with every other Qb.
3. At least one element of the set must be true.
4. All of the Qa have a common presupposition (i.e., there is a P such that for every Qa, Qa entails P).

Basically, these spaces are similar to what physicists call *state spaces*. A state space is a geometric representation of the possibilities of a system; a parametrization of its states, a display of its repertoire. In the case of a simple switch the state space has two elements:

$$\text{switch is} \left\{ \begin{array}{c} \text{on} \\ \text{off} \end{array} \right\}.$$

14. From *Josiah Royce's Seminar, 1913–14; as recorded in the Notebooks of Harry T. Costello,* ed. Grover Smith (New Brunswick, N.J.: Rutgers University Press, 1963), p. 137.

If such a switch is connected in a circuit with another switch, one which has, say, three positions (on, off, reversed), then the total state space for the complex system is the six-element product of the two:

$$\text{switch}_1 \text{ is } \left\{ \begin{array}{c} \text{on} \\ \text{off} \end{array} \right\} \qquad \times \qquad \text{switch}_2 \text{ is } \left\{ \begin{array}{c} \text{on} \\ \text{off} \\ \text{rev} \end{array} \right\}.$$

Such a space also represents the presuppositions of the explanation, in the sense that it makes clear how much is not being explained. For example, when the object of explanation is why the

$$\text{switch is } \left\{ \begin{array}{c} \text{on} \\ \text{off} \end{array} \right\},$$

the unvaried part gives us the presupposition. In this case it would include: what a switch is, why there is a switch here at all, why the switch has exactly those two positions, and so on.

Structural Presuppositions

There is a certain kind of presupposition that arises when the explanations we seek deal with individuals who are related in a larger system. The theory of these presuppositions is the foundation for much of what I am saying in this work.

Let me begin with an example. Suppose that, in a class I am teaching, I announce that the course will be "graded on a curve," that is, that I have decided beforehand what the overall distribution of grades is going to be. Let us say, for the sake of the example, that I decide that there will be one A, 24 B's, and 25 C's. The finals come in, and let us say Mary gets the A. She wrote an original and thoughtful final.

Now, if someone asks me why Mary got an A, I would say exactly what I just said: she wrote an original and throughtful final. Yet this is inadequate as it stands. Suppose *two* people had written finals that were well thought out and original. Would two people have received A's? Not if I am really grading on a curve. Because of this, it is misleading in a certain way to answer why Mary got an A by citing this simple fact about her—that she wrote a good final. It is misleading because it gives the impression that "writing a good final" is sufficient to explain "getting an A." But that is not true. Even if someone writes a good final, they may fail to get an A because someone else has written a *better* one. So it is more accurate to answer the question by pointing to the *relative* fact that Mary wrote the best paper in the class.

What is assumed here is something like:

Whoever writes the best final gets the A.

But if this is the general principle, we can see that a direct consequence of it is that exactly one person gets an A (since exactly one person can "write the best final"). There is, therefore, an unexplained presupposition that there is exactly one A in the class.

The nature of this presupposition distinguishes this case from cases in which there is no curve. In those cases, if Mary gets an A, even if she happens to be the only one to get one, we *can* answer the question

why Mary got an A

by citing factors that are purely about Mary and that contain no hidden presuppositions. In those sorts of situations the answer to the question about Mary would be something like:

She had taken a math course that was helpful

or

There was a big party the night before the final, but her phone was out of order,

or some answer from which it follows that had this been true of several people, then all of them could have received A's. In cases where there is no curve, we can explain each individual's fortune by appealing only to facts about that individual.

This fails, by definition, in the cases where there is a curve, for in those cases, there will be the unexplained presupposition, the presupposition of the grading structure, that in this case there will be exactly one A. This is also reflected in the fact that if we asked

Why didn't Bob get an A?

it would be legitimate to answer

because Mary's paper was better.

Here the presupposition is obvious.

Generally speaking, we can distinguish two different kinds of questions. The first is a question about the grade distribution or structure:

Why was there exactly one A?

The second kind of question presupposes the first and asks

What is it about Mary in virtue of which she got the A?

The first is a question about a distribution, the second is a question about an individual's place in that distribution.

The relation between these two kinds of questions is parallel to the Willie Sutton example. There we distinguished the two questions:

1. Why is there something (at all) which Sutton robs? (the priest's question)

and

2. Given that there is something which Sutton robs, why is it *banks*?

Similarly, in this case we can distinguish:

1. Why is there exactly one person getting an A?

and

2. Given that exactly one person is to get an A, why was it *Mary*?

Answers to the second question presuppose, and do not explain, answers to the first question. This is true even if we look at the individual explanations for everyone's performance. If we take each person in the class and ask why that person got the grade he or she did, we have fifty answers to the questions why

Mary got an A
Bob got a B

    .
    .
    .

Harold got a C

but the answers to those fifty questions do not add up to an answer to the question of why there was this distribution of grades.

Perhaps the clearest way to put this point is in terms of the contrast spaces of the two different explanations. If we look at the individuals, one by one, each individual has three possibilities: getting an A, getting a B, or getting a C. We can therefore represent a typical question as

$$\text{why Mary gets} \begin{Bmatrix} A \\ B \\ C \end{Bmatrix}.$$

Now the class is in some sense the sum of the individuals, and so it is natural to try, a priori, to represent the possibility-space of the whole class as the product of fifty copies of the individual possibility-space, one copy for each individual. This would give us a space for the whole class that was

$$S = \text{Mary gets} \begin{Bmatrix} A \\ B \\ C \end{Bmatrix} \times \text{Bob gets} \begin{Bmatrix} A \\ B \\ C \end{Bmatrix} \times \ldots \times \text{Harold gets} \begin{Bmatrix} A \\ B \\ C \end{Bmatrix}.$$

But this a priori possibility-space is not the true possibility-space of the class because it fails to take into account that certain combinations of individual possibilities are not collectively possible.

This *would* be the right space if the class were not graded on a curve. In the case where each individual's outcome depends only on facts about that individual, this is the true state space of the whole class. But in our example, the true possibility-space has far fewer than 3^{50} elements because a set of additional conditions has been imposed on the overall space. I will call these *structural* conditions. The effect of such conditions is to reduce, before any of the imagined contingencies, the number of possibilities (or "degrees of freedom") available to the system.

The true contrast space for the question about *Mary* consists of the number of ways a set of 50 people can be subdivided into a set of 1, a set of 24, and a set of 25, in other words, only those grade distributions consistent with my policy. The contrast is between those distributions in which Mary got the A and ones where someone else got the A. All other differences among distributions are irrelevant. Consequently, the true contrast space for that question is *not*:

$$\text{Why Mary got} \begin{Bmatrix} A \\ B \\ C \end{Bmatrix} \text{ but rather}$$

$$\text{Why} \begin{Bmatrix} \text{Mary} \\ \text{Bob} \\ . \\ . \\ . \\ \text{Harold} \end{Bmatrix} \text{ got the A.}$$

Writing the contrast space in this way makes it clear what is being presupposed by the questions about the individual's place in the distribution: they take the distribution itself as "given."

In the case of the structural question the situation is completely different. There the contrast would be between this grade distribution and the *other* possible grade distributions. The question "Why is there this distribution of grades?" contrasts this distribution with all the other possible distributions. Indeed, not only do the alternative possibilities include other grading *distributions* (5 A's, 20 B's, and so on), but for certain purposes one would have to include all other possible grading *policies*, even the nonstructured ones: giving no grades at all, giving A's to my friends, and so on.

In cases in which there is no predetermined distribution, the structural question

Why is there this distribution of grades?

does not really have a distinct answer. The answer to it is just that that's what the distribution of individual performances happened to be. If there are many C's, it is because many individuals happened to write poor papers. The question of the distribution collapses to the questions about the individuals. But where there is a predetermined policy, there is a separate nontrivial question about why that distribution was the case. What we are asking in those cases is not why there happened to be this distribution (e.g., one A) but rather why there *had* to be this distribution.

.   .   .

In cases like these, the imposed structural conditions radically alter the kinds of explanations we give because they constrain and truncate the contrast spaces. There is some precedent for this way of talking, and some good examples are to be found, in the state spaces of physics.

In analytical dynamics, the mathematical study of the physics of motion, these imposed conditions are called *kinematical conditions.*[15] Consider, for example, two mass points moving freely in a plane. The total state space of these two points has eight dimensions: two location coordinates and two velocity coordinates for each of the two particles. We

15. I take the term from Cornelius Lanczos's *The Variational Principles of Mechanics,* an excellent, and philosophically informed, treatment of analytical dynamics (Toronto: University of Toronto Press, 1949).

can then talk about their gravitational interactions by means of a differential equation in this eight-dimensional space. So far the particles are moving freely, and so there are as yet no kinematical conditions. But now suppose the two particles are joined together by a rigid rod. Then there are no longer eight degrees of freedom, for there is the restriction that the distance between the two particles is constant. This is a simple algebraic relation among some of the coordinates:

$$(x_1 - y_1)^2 + (x_2 - y_2)^2 = k^2,$$

where (x_1, x_2) and (y_1, y_2) are the position coordinates of the two particles. These four coordinates, or four dimensions, are not independent, since given any three we can compute the fourth. We could even use this equation to rewrite the basic dynamics by eliminating one of the variables, say x_1, and substituting its equivalent in terms of the other three position variables, thus leaving an equation which has explicitly only seven degrees of freedom.

One problem with doing this is that the kinematical condition is obviously symmetric in the four variables, and the choice of one of the variables to be replaced as a function of the others is therefore arbitrary and somewhat misleading. The analogue in the grading example would be to take one person in the class, say Harold, and to say that if we know the grades of the other 49 students we can determine Harold's grade; therefore, Harold can be eliminated as an independent variable. Why Harold? It is a more faithful representation of the situation to see it as an imposed relation among symmetric variables. (Indeed, one of the points of Lanczos's book is to argue that this way of treating it is much more natural than the asymmetric way and allows the use of powerful mathematical techniques.) Let me just list more examples of these kinematical conditions:

1. If the two particles are constrained to remain on the surface of a sphere, we have lost two degrees of freedom, since the four-dimensional space of possible positions has been reduced to the two-dimensional surface of the sphere.
2. Consider a lever. First view it as a system of material particles held together by a variety of intermolecular forces. Its state space is therefore of very high dimension, millions of degrees of freedom for the individual particles. But the fact that the lever is *rigid* means that a substantial kinematical condition has

been imposed, one which has the effect of reducing the degrees of freedom of the overall system from millions to exactly two: the location of one end-point and the angle of orientation.

3. (An example from social science.) Consider two people involved in what is called a *zero-sum game.* In such a game, one player's wins are at the expense of the other. The state space of such a game would involve points representing the moves available to each player, and the outcomes dependent on them. The competitive or zero-sum nature of the game is then expressed by the imposed kinematical condition:

$$x_1 + x_2 = 0,$$

where x_1 is the payoff to the first player, and x_2 is the payoff to the second player.

The important point is this: the existence of such kinematical conditions makes it possible to make explanations within the system a lot more simply than we might be able to do otherwise. This is because when such conditions exist, the complexity of the explanation can be greatly reduced. For example, in the case of the lever, suppose it is in equilibrium with certain weights at certain points on it. In order to explain this in the very high dimensional state space of its constituent particles, we would have to know the representation of the state of the lever and its weights in that multidimensional space. The explanation, having literally millions of dimensions, would be awesomely complicated. But the assumption of rigidity enables us to reduce this complexity to a manageable level. What is more, if we were to try to explain a particular equilibrium in the particle-space, *we would even have to know the nature of the underlying intermolecular forces* that are responsible for the rigidity. The kinematical approach enables us to finesse this problem.

Similarly, in the case of the zero-sum game, the kinematical condition enables us to pare down explanations. In order to explain why the payoff to the two players was (a, b), it suffices to give a one-dimensional explanation because the thing to be explained is, appearances to the contrary, only one dimensional: we know "a priori" that $b = -a$.

We might say, in the case of the zero-sum game, that we can explain why, given that there is a zero sum, it is *this* pair of values and not that, e.g., why it is $(6, -6)$ rather than $(9, -9)$. But we cannot, on this possibility-space, explain why there is a zero sum at all, because every possible causal antecedent produces some zero sum or other. Thus it is like the grading example.

.   .   .

To summarize, explanations have presuppositions which, among other things, limit drastically the alternatives to the thing being explained. These presuppositions radically affect the success and failure of potential explanations and the interrelation of various explanations. Call this *explanatory relativity*.

A perspicuous way to represent this phenomenon is the device of contrast spaces, or spaces of live alternatives. The structure of these spaces displays some of the presuppositions of a given explanation.

One particular class of examples of explanatory relativity is especially worth noting: cases where a system consists of a number of individuals, each with its own individual possibility-space, but where the true possibility-space of the total system is not the full product of the individual spaces. In such cases the presuppositions (analogous to kinematical conditions) establish internal relations among the individuals, and in such cases explanations of individual properties will take a very special form. Moreover, such explanations (e.g., why *Mary* got an A) always presuppose, and hence can never explain, the overall structure of the system.

I now want to go on to apply these remarks in a study of various kinds of reductionism.

2 Reductionism

Reduction

Reductionist claims are often expressed by saying that something "is just" (or "is really") something else.

The claim that psychology is reducible to physics or chemistry is expressed as the statement that people "are just" physical objects. The claim that actions are reducible to primitive drives is put as the statement that human behavior "is just" the expression of those drives. There are claims that everything "is just" economics, while others say that everything "is just" biology. The claim that thermodynamics is reducible to statistical mechanics is expressed as the claim that a gas "is just" a collection of molecules, and the claim that social laws are reducible to the actions of individuals is expressed as the claim that society "is just" individuals.

The first problem with such claims is understanding what they could possibly mean. What does it mean to say that something "is just" (or "is really") something else?

The examples suggest that what is being claimed is a certain fact about *explanation*, namely, that the phenomena of the first kind are explainable from the theory of the second kind. The reducibility of psychology to physics and chemistry amounts to the claim that conduct can be explained wholly in terms of physical and chemical phenomena. Similarly in each of the other cases, the claim is that the one theory explains the other phenomena.

So reduction, which is on its face an ontological question, is really a question about the possibility of explanation: to say that something is reducible to something else is to say that certain kinds of explanations exist. This can be reconciled with more traditional conceptions, perhaps the best known of which is Quine's "ontological reduction." On his view an ontological reduction has been effected when one realm of discourse has been shown to be eliminable in favor of another:

We have, to begin with, an expression or form of expression that is
somehow troublesome. . . . But it also serves other purposes that are
not to be abandoned. Then we find a way of accomplishing these same
purposes through other channels, using other and less troublesome
forms of expression. The old perplexities are solved.[1]

So one theory reduces another if it enables us to "accomplish the
same purposes" as the other. Reducibility becomes relativized to a set
of purposes. But there are some purposes for which almost any theory
can replace any other (e.g., in serving as an exercise in penmanship)
and other purposes for which nothing else will do. Therefore the question of reducibility turns on what the crucial purposes are, and here
Quine does not really tell us which we should insist on and which we
should forgo. His pragmatism takes the purposes on which everything
turns to be uncontroversial, given from the outside, or at any rate not
themselves problematic. He does not offer a theory of what our purposes should be.

If we supply the missing purpose as explanation, the resulting account
of reduction corresponds to our own: one realm of discourse is reducible
to another if the reduction theory gives us all the explanatory power
of the theory being reduced.

This gives us a criterion for assessing a reduction. Look at the explanations that are possible in the one realm of discourse and see whether we
can explain the same phenomena in the other. If we can, the reduction
is successful.

It is very important to note that this criterion depends on its being
clear what "the same phenomena" are. But often we do not know when
one term in one theory and another term in another are referring to
the same phenomenon. If psychology speaks of "aggression" as hostility
toward imagined castration, and sociobiology speaks of "aggression"
as biological territoriality, is this the same phenomenon? It is not clear.

So in order to assess a claim of reduction, we need a notion of when
two explanations are explaining the same thing. This was already
mentioned in the introduction, but we can now give that notion a little
more content by using the machinery of chapter 1. In particular we can
say that if the reduction is to be successful, the two explanations must
have the same *object*. This means that they must be about the same
phenomena and also that they must construe the problematic in the

1. W. V. Quine, *Word and Object* (Cambridge: M.I.T. Press, 1960), p. 260.

same way. Not only must they be talking about the same thing (e.g., Sutton's bank robbing) but they must have contrast spaces that line up in the right way (as Sutton's and the priest's do not). Otherwise the reduction will fail.

This gives us a simple test to apply to reductions: Do their objects correspond? My strategy will be to assess various claims of reduction by studying their objects, especially with respect to the relevant contrast spaces.

Microreduction: The Whole and Its Parts

I want to focus on one particular archetype of reduction: the reduction which is said to hold between a whole and its parts, between an object and the stuff or things which comprise it. In such claims, called *microreductions,* a certain object can be explained as just the sum of its parts. In microreduction the upper level object is explainable by the (lower level) microtheory. Therefore, the upper-level explanations can in principle be eliminated in favor of the microexplanations.

The classic manifesto of microreduction was the 1958 paper by Oppenheim and Putnam, "Unity of Science as a Working Hypothesis."[2] It laid out seven levels of scientific phenomena. The objects at each level contain as their parts the objects of the next lower level. The level of the biology of the organism has as its objects whole organisms, which are composed of the objects of the next lower level, cells. Cells, in turn, are composed of biochemical molecules, which are in turn composed of atoms. The thesis of the "unity of science" is that each level is reducible to the next lower: organism biology to cell biology, cell biology to biochemistry, biochemistry to physics, and so forth.

But what does *reducible* mean? The notion they use is in some ways like ours. They say that theory A is reducible to theory B if B explains all the observation sentences that A does. This is like our criterion in holding that the successful reduction enables us to recapture explanations. It differs in having a specific notion of what the objects of explanation are: observation sentences. Their use of this notion comes from basic empiricism: a theory is divided into a "theoretical vocabulary" and an "observation vocabulary," with the observation vocabulary confronting experience directly. Because only observation

2. In H. Feigel, M. Scriven, and G. Maxwell, eds., *Minnesota Studies in the Philosophy of Science,* vol. 2 (Minneapolis: University of Minnesota Press, 1955).

statements had any transtheoretical cash value, if one theory captured all the observation statements of another, it captured all that was worth capturing and hence had achieved a successful reduction.

There are several problems with this view. The first stems from the idea that it is a *sentence,* a piece of syntax, that is the object of explanation. The problem is that looking at sentences will not tell you whether two sentences are talking about the same thing. If a term X appears in theory A, and a term X appears in theory B, and theory B explains all the sentences in which X occurs, is it a successful reduction? It will be only if the two terms X are really the same, that is, if they both *refer* to the same phenomenon. This means that we cannot limit ourselves to talking about the terms in question but must go beyond them to talk about that to which the terms refer, the phenomena themselves.

The second weakness of the positivist approach is the reliance on *observation.* Even if theory B explained all the observation sentences that theory A does, its status as a reduction would be in doubt unless it could also explain the mechanisms and postulated unobservables, the explaining entities, of theory A.[3]

If we negate these two aspects, we arrive at a more realist notion of reduction. This realist version of the Oppenheim–Putnam criterion would then correspond to the one I am proposing: that theory A is reducible to theory B if theory B explains the phenomena previously the province of theory A.

Taking this as our definition of reduction, we can return to the claims of microreduction, the reduction of the upper level to the underlying level, and ask, What reason are we given for thinking that the explanations of each level are reducible to the explanations of the underlying level? The answer is: not much. The authors really did think of it as a "working hypothesis" and were more concerned to evoke a method and show some examples than to give an argued presentation. In fact, arguments in this area seem hard to find. Most reductionists rely on the assertion that the underlying level is "all there really is," or that "there isn't anything but . . . ," or they warn that the denial of reductionism is somehow "mysterious," a belief in a holistic ecto-

3. For this point see Richard Boyd, "Realism, Undetermination and a Causal Theory of the Evidence," *Nous* 7 (1973): 1, and his *Realism and Scientific Epistemology* (New York: Cambridge University Press, forthcoming).

plasm. Thus the economist Kenneth Arrow writes of reduction in social theory:

> A full characterization of each individual's behavior logically implies a knowledge of group behavior; there is nothing left out. The rejection of the organism approach to social problems has been a fairly complete, and to my mind salutary, rejection of mysticism.[4]

The reductionist's claim, then, is that the lower-level description is somehow all there is; such a description is complete. We can express this as a pair of slogans:

1. for every state, a microstate;

and

2. for every microstate, a microexplanation.

In other words the claim is that the microlevel constitutes an *underlying determinism,* a complete causal picture. So far, so good, we think.

Let us suppose that there is indeed such an underlying determinism. To every upper-level state (macrostate) there corresponds a microstate, and for every microstate, there is a microexplanation. The question is, Does this imply that the explanations of the macrolevel are in any sense dispensable or reducible? I will argue that the answer is no.

We need a concrete example to use as a focus for this discussion, and I will use one from population ecology. Suppose we have an ecological system composed of foxes and rabbits. There are periodic fluctuations in the population levels of the two species, and the explanation turns out to be that the foxes eat the rabbits to such a point that there are too few rabbits left to sustain the fox population, so the foxes begin dying off. After a while, this takes the pressure off the rabbits, who then begin to multiply until there is plenty of food for the foxes, who begin to multiply, killing more rabbits, and so forth.

We can construct a simple global model of this process by taking as our basic variables the levels of the fox and rabbit populations:

$X(t)$ = level of fox population at time t.

$Y(t)$ = level of rabbit population at time t.

The main influences on the levels of the populations will be the frequency with which foxes encounter, and eat, rabbits. The number of

4. "Mathematical Models in the Social Sciences" in M. Brodbeck, ed., *Readings in the Philosophy of the Social Sciences* (New York: Macmillan, 1968), p. 641.

encounters between foxes and rabbits will clearly be proportional both
to the fox level and to the rabbit level. We use as an estimate the
product, XY. This frequency of encounter will appear as a positive contribution to the fox level and as a negative contribution to the rabbit
level. The fox level is also affected by the number of foxes itself because
the more foxes there are, the more competition there is. So the dynamics of the fox level can be represented by the ordinary differential
equation

$$\frac{dX}{dt} = aXY - bX,$$

which represents the sum of these two contributions. On the other
hand, the rabbit level is determined by the frequency of encounter
(negatively) and by the proverbial multiplication of rabbits (positively),
so its law is

$$\frac{dY}{dt} = cY - dXY.$$

Jointly, these two determine a two-dimensional ordinary differential
equation on the two-dimensional state space of population levels.[5]

Using this law or its ordinary language versions, we can then frame
explanations for various phenomena. First of all, there is the basic
explanation for the fluctuations which we saw above and various other
explanations which derive from it. For example, if the fox population
is high, this will place great pressure on the rabbits, and when one of
them gets caught and eaten, it is reasonable to say:

> The cause of the death of the rabbit was that the fox population
> was high.

This seems like an acceptable explanation although its form is that of
an explanation of a microstate, the death of a rabbit, by appeal to

5. This is called the *Lotka-Volterra* equation. The classic sources are A. J.
Lotka, *Elements of Mathematic Biology* (Baltimore: Williams and Wilkins, 1925),
and V. Volterra, *Leçons sur la théorie mathématique de la lutte pour la vie*
(Paris: Gauthier-Villars, 1931). Two contemporary treatments are Braun, *Differential Equations and Their Applications* (New York: Springer-Verlag, 1975),
and E. C. Pielou, *An Introduction to Mathematical Ecology* (New York: Wiley-
Interscience, 1977). These works present the relevant biological and mathematical
reasoning but do not draw philosophical conclusions.

another macrostate, the level of the fox population. Similarly, statements like

The cause of the low level of the rabbit population is the high level of foxes,

involve an explanation of a macrostate by appeal to another macrostate. So these are typical explanations from the upper level. Reductionism tells us that these can be eliminated in terms of microexplanations. Well, *which* ones?

Consider first the case of the explanation of the death of the rabbit. We are told that since this is a microstate we must look on the microlevel for its explanation. What do we see when we look there? Presumably, something like this: Rabbit r, hopping through the field one afternoon, passed closely, too closely, to a tree behind which fox f was lurking and so got eaten. The microexplanation is therefore something like

Rabbit r was eaten because he passed through the capture space of fox f,

because the overall nature of the microlevel is a huge-dimensional determinism, which, given a complete description of all the equations of interaction between individual foxes and individual rabbits (depending on such things as their physiology and reaction times) and given a complete specification of an initial distribution of foxes and rabbits, tells us the individual destiny of every one of them at every future time. Extracting from this mass the data relevant to rabbit r, we learn that, given certain initial positions and other factors, it follows that rabbit r was to pass through the capture space of fox f. This is our microexplanation.

The problem of reductionism is therefore: Do microexplanations such as this enable us to dispense with macroexplanations? This turns on what these explanations are really explanations *of*, in the sense of the previous chapter. When we consider this, we can see that their respective objects do not really correspond. The first explanation, for example, cited the high fox population as the cause of the death of the rabbit, and "the death of the rabbit" was also the microobject. But this is not really true; the actual object of the microexplanation is not

the death of the rabbit,

but rather

the death of the rabbit at the hands of fox f, at place *p*, time *t,* and
so on.

The microlevel has an extremely specific object of explanation and consequently an extremely specific antecedent to explain it. But we do not
really want to know why the rabbit was eaten by that fox at that time
and under those circumstances; we want to know why he was eaten (period). The object of the macroexplanation is why

the rabbit was $\begin{Bmatrix} \text{eaten} \\ \text{not eaten} \end{Bmatrix}$,   *at a period of time*

while all the microexplanation tells us is why

the rabbit was eaten $\begin{Bmatrix} \text{by fox f at time } t \dots \\ \text{by some other fox} \dots \end{Bmatrix}$.

The microexplanation, therefore, contains much that is irrelevant to why
the rabbit got eaten and does not really answer that question at all.
There are several reasons for insisting on the autonomy of the higher-
order question of why the rabbit got eaten. Obviously, there are pragmatic considerations recommending it. What the rabbit wants to know
is why rabbits get eaten, not why they get eaten by specific foxes. It is
the higher-order explanation which provides the information that is of
value to the rabbit. It is more valuable because if the circumstances had
been slightly different, then, although the rabbit would not have been
eaten by fox f, he probably (assuming the high fox population) would
have been eaten by another fox. The microexplanation does not tell us
this and does not tell us how sensitive the outcome is to changes in the
conditions. Therefore, it does not tell us what things would have to be
otherwise for the rabbit *not* to get eaten.

This difference makes the macroobject superior to the microobject in
several ways. The first is pragmatic. The microexplanation includes data
that are irrelevant to the outcome and therefore bury the explanation
unrecognizably. It delivers an embarrassment of riches and so is less useful. It also does not lend itself to a certain kind of practical reasoning,
which the macroexplanation does. In many cases the point of asking for
an explanation of something is that we are interested in eradicating or
preventing it. Microexplanations, by their nature, cannot lend themselves to this use.

as a whole or at a particular time

The difference between the micro- and macroexplanations is not only
pragmatic. It centers on the requirement that an explanation tell us *what*

could have been otherwise. This requirement has several sources. In addition to the pragmatic factors there are considerations from what could be called the pure theory of causality which suggest such a requirement. Basically, they stem from the idea that a causal explanation has as much to do with what is causally necessary as with what is causally sufficient. This conception of causality is gaining currency, and several contemporary philosophers have proposed an analysis of causation in terms of a negative counterfactual, the same kind I have been recommending for "practical" reasons.[6]

These difficulties of the microexplanation are related to the requirement discussed in the previous chapter, that an explanation must have a certain amount of *stability* under perturbations of its conditions. Recall the discussion of the auto accident example: I argued that

auto accident at x, t, . . .

was not a good choice of object of explanation for the auto accident because it was extremely unstable under small perturbations. The crucial point there, as here, is: If things had been otherwise, what would have happened?

In both cases structural factors operate to ensure the stability of the object at the macrolevel. We know that the rabbit started out at place p and did certain things which led to its being eaten. But if it had not done those things, it would have done other things which also would have resulted in its being eaten. This often happens in the explanation of social phenomena. We may explain why a child has certain attitudes by pointing out that it had certain experiences. This teacher said that to them on such-and-such day, they saw such-and-such movie, all of which had the effect of engendering a certain attitude. But if the attitude is relatively important to a society, the means of generating that attitude will not be left to chance; there will be a multiplicity, a *redundancy,* of mechanisms to ensure that the child developed the "right" attitude.

So the causality with which the effect is produced has a strong resiliency. The very fact that the child did not have those experiences calls forth other experiences to do the job of producing the effect. The same is true in the foxes and rabbits case: the very fact that the rabbit did not wander into the capture space of fox f makes it likely that it will be eaten by another fox.

6. See the discussion on p. 163.

I want to call this "redundant causality." Systems which exhibit redundant causality therefore have, for every consequent Q, a bundle of antecedents (P_i) such that:

1. If any one of the P_i is true, so will be Q.
2. If one P_i should not be the case, some other will.

Obviously, in any system with redundant causality, citing the actual P_i that caused Q will be defective as an explanation. This will apply to many cases in which P_i is the microexplanation.

The motivation of reductionism then becomes clearer. If some structural fact is responsible for a redundant causality producing Q, then, as I said, it will be misleading to cite the P_i which actually occurred as the explanation of Q. But *some P_i* did have to occur. The macroexplanation tells us that some realization or other will be the case to bring about Q but is indifferent as to which. The microexplanation tells us the mechanism by which the macroexplanation operated. The structure gives the *why*, while the microexplanation gives the *how*.

We can see the force behind the reductionist's claim. Without some mechanism or other, without some realization of the effectivity of the structure, it really would be mysterious to talk about the structure's *causing* something. But merely citing the specific mechanism which brought about the effect does not tell us the important fact that had that particular mechanism not occurred, then some other would have, to accomplish the same end.[7] The crucial point here is that the particular mechanism was not necessary for the effect, and therefore it is not a good explanation to cite it as the cause.

And so, even if such underlying determinisms do exist, we need more than them in order to get an explanation. Miccroreduction is sometimes thought of as an ideal, something that is possible "in theory" though not "in practice." One can then be a reductionist while conceding a "practical" independence. But my claim is stronger than that: the explanations we want simply do not exist at the underlying level. It is not that the microreduction is an impractical ideal, too good to be true, but rather that it is, in a way, too true to be good.

---

7. Such systems act as if they are goal directed because, should one means to the end be blocked, the system will shift to an alternative.

Explanation Seeks Its Own Level

So the fact that something materially "is" something else does not mean that we can reduce the explanations involved.[8] From the point of view of explanation there is a relative independence from the nature of the substrate. A macrostate, a higher level state of the organization of a thing, or a state of the social relations between one thing and another can have a particular realization which, in some sense, "is" that state in this case. But the explanation of the higher order state will not proceed via the microexplanation of the microstate which it happens to "be." Instead, the explanation will seek its own level, and typically this will not be the level of the underlying substratum. The level on which it occurs will be whatever one has the redundancies and structural factors that make nontrivial explanation possible.

A number of different approaches to explanation share the assumption that explanation can be liberated from the nature of the substratum. For example, it is one of the fundamental themes of structuralism, characteristic of Saussure's work on sign systems and Lévi-Strauss's analyses of societies. Both try to find elementary structures, binary oppositions, for example, that occur in all different kinds of matter. The explanations given are in terms of the forms themselves and not in terms of the kind of thing which happens to be realizing this form.

It has recently become a theme in the writing of the mathematician René Thom. In an article called "Structuralism and Biology" he writes:

> A knowledge of the fine structure, molecules for a fluid, cells for an animal, is practically irrelevant for understanding the global structure . . . of the total system. For instance, the final structure of a theory like Fluid Mechanics does not depend on whether one takes as the basic concept molecules or a continuous fluid.[9]

But the independence of levels of explanation is not limited to structuralists in any narrow sense; it can be found in Aristotle's remark that in explanation it is the form and not the matter that counts, or in Russell's remark that in mathematics we do not know what we are talking about. In each case its role is to license some form of anti-

8. It follows that the "is" of material identity is not the "is" of reduction.
9. In C. H Waddington, ed., *Towards a Theoretical Biology* (Edinburgh: Edinburgh University Press, 1972), p. 78.

reductionism. What the particular subject matter is varies from case to case. It may be anything from fluid mechanics, as above, to music. Schoenberg took an antireductionist approach to music theory, where the independence of levels of explanation takes the form of an independence of the theory of harmony from the fine structure of the physics of tone:

> Should someone succeed in deriving the phenomena solely from the physical properties of tone and explaining them solely on that basis, then it would hardly matter whether our physical knowledge of the nature of tone is correct or not. It is entirely possible that in spite of an observation falsely construed as fundamental we may, by inference or through intuition, arrive at correct results; whereas it is not at all a proved fact that more correct or better observation would necessarily yield a more correct or better conclusion.[10]

One area in which this kind of antireductionism has been especially important is the question of the reducibility of human activity to biology. Here, reductionism takes the form of a claim that human action "is just" neurophysiology. So in order to assess this claim, we have to ask: Even if the actions have a neurophysiological substratum, will neurophysiology *explain* them?

In the *Phaedo* (99 E ff.), Socrates says no. The reason he gives is that the neurophysiological account ("nerves and bones and sinew"), although presumably true, does not give us an explanation (aitia) of human action. A true explanation must inevitably be in terms of *reasons,* not "nerves and bones and sinew." The latter are the necessary medium of any human action, but citing them does not suffice to explain action, because, he says, it does not explain why he does one thing (staying in jail) rather than another (escaping).

Recently, the same kind of independence of explanation has been argued against the identification of mental states with physical states. Hilary Putnam, in a series of papers, argues that mental states cannot be reduced to their material realizations in this or that organism. "Pain," for example, denotes a *functional* state, a relatively high-order property of the organization of a creature. The specific mechanisms which realize pain in one kind of organism (say, with a carbon-based biochemistry) may be very different from the ways that pain is realized in another kind or organism (say, with a silicon-based chemistry), or for

10. A. Schoenberg, *Theory of Harmony* (Berkeley: University of California Press, 1978), p. 42.

that matter, the ways that pain is realized in some artificially created machine. Therefore the explanations which pain enters into (like "he cried out from the pain" or "the wound caused great pain") must be captured on the appropriate level, which in this case means the level of functional organization. It is a mistake, a kind of hyperspecificity, to try to explain this in terms of the specific mechanisms which realize pain in this particular creature. Hence statements about pain (or preferences) in various machines "are not logically equivalent to statements concerning the physical-chemical composition of these machines."[11] These explanations seek their own level.

Freeing explanation from the substrate produces new strategies of explanation, strategies which depend on the autonomy of levels. Perhaps the most sweeping approach of this sort is the one which the mathematician Thom has proposed as a new model for scientific explanation. He begins by rejecting reductionism:

> [The] ancient dream of the atomist—to reconstruct the universe and all its properties in one theory of combinations of elementary particles and their interactions—has scarcely been started (e.g., there is no satisfactory theory of the liquid state of matter).

As an alternative program, he suggests:

> If the biologist is to progress and to understand living processes, he cannot wait until physics and chemistry can give him a complete theory of all local phenomena found in living matter; instead, he should try only to construct a model that is locally compatible with known properties of the environment and to separate off the geometricoalgebraic structure ensuring the stability of the system, without attempting a complete description of living matter. This methodology goes against the present dominant philosophy that the first step in revealing nature must be the analysis of the system and its ultimate constituents. We must reject this primitive and almost cannibalistic delusion about knowledge, that an understanding of something requires first that we dismantle it, like a child who pulls a watch to pieces and spreads out the wheels in order to understand the mechanism.[12]

11. "The Mental Life of Some Machines," p. 420. A good account of antireductionism in the philosophy of mind can be found in W. A. Wimsatt, "Reductionism, Levels of Organization, and the Mind–Body Problem," in G. Globus, *Brain and Mind* (New York: Plenum, 1976).

12. *Structural Stability and Morphogenesis* (New York: W. A. Benjamin, 1975), p. 159.

Against Reduction
What all these approaches have in common is a style of explanation in
which explanations of the upper-level phenomena proceed independently
of any reduction. The idea is that no matter what the substratum turns
out to be, we can proceed independently to construct upper-level explanations. So far, this is a fairly modest claim. It asserts only a declara-
tion of independence for explanations. Most sober antireductionists
stop at this assertion.

I want to make a stronger claim: that in many cases, the microlevel
is inadequate, and we therefore *must* construct upper-level explanations. For this stronger claim, we need more than examples and plau-
sibility arguments. My argument for the indispensability of upper-level
explanations rests on a conception of what an explanation is.

In the second section (Microreduction: The Whole and Its Parts) of
this chapter we saw one basic argument against microreduction: that
microreduction fails as an explanation because its object is too specific.
This hyperconcreteness, for example, in choosing

the death of the rabbit at the hands of fox f at place x at time
t, . . .

as the object of explanation has the consequence that the resulting
explanation gives us a false picture of the sensitivity of the situation
to change. It suggests that, had the specific cause not been the case,
the effect would not have occurred. This is false in such cases because
there is a redundant causality operating, the effect of which is to
ensure that many *other* states, perturbations of the original microcause,
would have produced the same result. Microreductions cannot take
account of this redundancy and to that extent cannot replace upper-
level explanations.

Consider the case of reducing human action to neurophysiology. Here
reductionism says that the action of raising my arm "is just" the
physical movement of the arm (the underlying state), together with
its microexplanation (the neurophysiological causes of the movement
of the arm). But the problem with such an identification is that we
do not *want* an explanation of why my arm moved in *exactly* that way.
Suppose my arm moved in some specific trajectory T. Then the underlying determinism explains why my arm moved precisely in trajectory T.
But any such explanation will contain much that is irrelevant to why
I moved my arm because the object

I moved my arm

is much more general, much more stable, than the object

my arm moved in trajectory *T*.

My arm did not have to move in exactly that trajectory for it to have been the same action, and thus an explanation of that specific trajectory will be subject to the same objections as the explanations we saw earlier of why the rabbit was eaten by *that* fox or why I had *that* (very) auto accident. In each case the stability of the upper-level object under perturbations of the microstate demands an autonomous level of explanation appropriate to its own object. If, for example, the explanation of why my arm moved is that I was shaking hands with someone to whom I was being introduced, this explanation gives us what the underlying neurophysiology does not: a conception of what the allowable variation in the circumstances might have been.

This is worth examining in greater detail. In each of these cases there is an underlying substratum with its own local determinism, the principles that explain the causal succession of the microstates. For each microstate Y_0, we have another microstate X_0 and a microexplanation of Y_0 in terms of X_0. Such explanations are deficient in being hyperspecific. The occurrence of the specific microstate X_0 was not necessary for the occurrence of the qualitative outcome, and hence it is counterexplanatory to include it in the explanation.

But, of course, not *all* perturbations of the underlying state produce the same outcome. *Some* will result in a qualitatively different outcome. It is crucial for the upper-level explanation that we get some account of what things really are relevant to the outcome. The underlying determinism also fails to supply this. It has no account of the sensitive aspects of the causal connection.

And that is, after all, what we really want to know: what is going to make a difference? Along what dimensions is the outcome *un*stable, that is, sensitive to variations in the underlying state?

We can imagine the space of the substratum as underlying the whole process. We have a complete set of microstates and a principle of microexplanation, V, which explains the microstate Y_0 in terms of X_0:

$$X_0 \xrightarrow{V} Y_0.$$

The rabbit was eaten by fox f ($= Y_0$) because it was at a certain place, time, and so on ($= X_0$). For most X_0, this evolution is smooth; small changes in X_0 do not make for qualitative changes. But at certain critical points, small perturbations *do* make a difference and will result in the rabbit's wandering out of the capture space of the fox. These critical points mark the boundaries of the regions of smooth change. They partition the underlying space into equivalence classes within which the map is stable. The crucial thing we want to know is how this set of critical points is embedded in the substratum space, for that will tell us what is really relevant and what is not. Therefore, what is necessary for a true explanation is an account of how the underlying space is partitioned into basins of irrelevant differences, separated by ridge lines of critical points.[13]

Consider an example. A car is stopped at a traffic light. The light changes, and the car proceeds. Now try to visualize this episode purely from the point of view of the underlying physics. The picture looks like this. We had a steady, stable distribution of mass and energy. Then there was a small change in the energy distribution (the light changing), a variation which was, from the physical point of view, negligible. This tiny variation then produced an enormous effect: a large mass was set into motion.

In other words the underlying physics gives us a physical relation:

$$\left\{ \begin{matrix} \text{red} \\ \text{green} \end{matrix} \right\} \quad \text{light} \Longrightarrow \text{car} \quad \left\{ \begin{matrix} \text{stops} \\ \text{goes} \end{matrix} \right\}.$$

Along most of its parameters this is a stable relationship. Small changes in the intensity of the light or its shape will not produce a qualitatively different outcome. There is, however, one dimension along which it is unstable: the red–green boundary.

The fact that there is such an instability means that we cannot simply cite the underlying physics as the explanation for the car's stopping or

13. This is the basic picture of Thom's *catastrophe theory*. See his *Structural Stability and Morphogenesis* for an account of catastrophes. Two good works on the mathematical foundations are M. Golubitsky and V. Guillemin, *Stable Mappings and Their Singularities* (New York: Springer-Verlag, 1973), and Y. C. Lu, *Singularity Theory and an Introduction to Catastrophe Theory* (New York: Springer-Verlag, 1976). A good popular account can be found in A. Woodcock and M. Davis, *Catastrophe Theory* (E. P. Dutton: New York, 1978). The basic picture stems ultimately from Poincaré's contribution to the problem of the stability of the solar system, for which see R. Abraham and J. Marsden, *Foundations of Mechanics* (Reading, Mass.: Benjamin/Cummings, 1978).

going. What we must supply in addition is an account of why these instabilities occur; this is something which is imposed on the underlying substratum not something which arises from it.

Discontinuities and instabilities mean that purely mechanical explanation fails at that point, and we must show why the qualitative outcome occurred by showing how the upper level partitions the underlying set of physical signals into two equivalence classes, "red light" and "green light." All red lights are equivalent to all others, and, conversely, all red lights are radically different from all green lights despite their physical similarity. So the underlying space is partitioned into equivalence classes within which differences do not make a difference but across which differences *do* make a difference.

This means that there is some kind of discontinuity in the underlying space. In the natural topology on the space of physical signals, the map from the signal input to the action output is discontinuous on the boundary between red and green.[14]

The resulting picture of qualitative changes intervening in an underlying determinism is a very attractive and useful one. Thom and his followers have already applied it to physical examples such as phase transitions, for example, liquid to gas, where the smooth relationships among pressure, volume, and temperature become discontinuous at the boundaries which mark the transitions from one phase to the other. Another example of Thom's is embryological development, in which each phase of development features smooth and continuous change, punctuated by symmetry-breaking changes that introduce new morphologies, new qualitative stages.

It is especially tempting to try to apply this picture to the development and change of large-scale social forms. Feudalism, mercantilism, the capitalism of small traders, and the capitalism of oligopolies would become phases in the morphological development of society, separated by revolutionary (sudden or gradual) phase transitions.

It is difficult at this point to say whether this picture has any real content. The phases of social history seem to lend themselves to this kind of dynamical description. Marx spoke of revolution as like the

14. This is very much in the spirit of Thom. In his view every underlying space is stratified into regions within which there are no qualitative changes. The regions are separated by a boundary, called the catastrophe set, across which changes in parameters produce qualitative changes in the form of the outcome. The catastrophe set is just the set of singularities of the underlying map.

change from water to steam. Henry Adams, fascinated with Gibbs phase rule, which limits the number and kinds of phase changes that can occur in physical systems, made analogous claims about the phases in the development of Western thought (see "The Rule of Phase Applied to History" in his *The Degradation of the Democratic Dogma*).

It seems possible that such a program, a qualitative dynamics of history, can be carried out, perhaps even far enough to satisfy the conjecture of Thomas Pynchon:

> If tensor analysis is good enough for turbulence, it ought to be good enough for history. There ought to be nodes, critical points . . . there ought to be super-derivatives of the crowded and insatiate flow that can be set equal to zero and these critical points found . . . 1904 was one of them.[15]

·   ·   ·

To summarize, we began this discussion by considering the nature of reduction as a general claim about explanations. Specifically, we considered the claims of microreduction, that the underlying level is in some sense "all there really is." The notion of contrast spaces and the related concept of the object of explanation was then brought to bear: Do the upper-level theory and the would-be reduction have the same object of explanation? My answer was no. They generally have distinct objects; this, in turn, means that for certain basic purposes the underlying level cannot replace the upper-level theory.

I now want to extend the discussion by considering a very special class of cases of reductionism, the discussion of which takes up the rest of this work. It is the class of reductions in which the underlying level is *atomistic*, that is, in which the upper level is an aggregate of microindividuals, whose interaction is supposed to produce the upper-level phenomena.

Atomism
Let us therefore consider microreductions in which the underlying level is a collection of *atoms*. The term "atom" is meant here not in the narrow sense but as including all cases in which there is an aggregation of many similar individual entities, with the upper level said to arise from their interaction.

In such cases the overall structure appears as follows. We have, on

15. *Gravity's Rainbow* (New York: Viking Press, 1973), p. 451.

the one hand, the atoms. Each atom has a nature, a possibility-space which is taken as initially given. Then we imagine many of these atoms being collected into the overall system, so that the possibility-space of the total system is the sum (the Cartesian product) of the possibility-spaces of the atomic constituents.

As a general style of explanation, atomism dates from Leucippus and Democritus. Aristotle criticizes atomism in the *De Generatione* and in the *Metaphysics*.[16] In its modern form it appeared as methodological doctrine in the seventeenth century. Most explicit was Hobbes, who based his political philosophy on atomism as a method of knowledge, a philosophy of science: "It is necessary that we know the things that are to be compounded before we can know the whole compound, (for) everything is best understood by its constitutive causes."[17] It received a tremendous impetus from the work of Newton, whose derivation of the elliptical orbits of the planets stands as one of the great paradigms of atomist reductionism. He showed that, given two "atoms," in this case, gravitational mass-points, with an individual "nature," given by the laws of motion and the law of universal gravitation, the overall system of elliptical orbits could be deduced and thereby explained.

This reduction served as the (conscious or unconscious) paradigm for much of the intellectual life of the seventeenth and eighteenth centuries. It had a tremendous impact even on social theory, as we will see in the next chapter, but its influence was very broad. It is hard for us to imagine the force of its impact. The basic form of his explanation became the ideal toward which all explanation strived. We have nothing in the modern era to compare it with; no discovery or theory has spread to other fields or captured the general imagination the way Newton did.[18]

My interest here is in atomism as it functions in social theory, that is, in the doctrines of *individualism*. But I do not mean to suggest that individualism in social theory is simply the result of the application of the Newtonian paradigm. For one thing, this would be historically inaccurate. Hobbes's *Leviathan* was published in 1651, Newton's *Principia* in

16. Vide *De Gen* I and *Met.* 1071 b 33.
17. *English Works of Thomas Hobbes,* vol. 1, p. 67; vol. 2, p. xiv (citation from Lukes, *Individualism,* p. 110).
18. Compare it, e.g., to the theory of relativity, whose cultural impact, so far, is limited to certain undergraduates who now think they have Einstein's blessing for thinking that "everything is relative" (and to whom it is useful to point that the fundamental postulate of the theory is that the speed of light is absolute).

1687. But more important, Hobbes did not merely take a picture from physics and apply it to society. His atomism is as much a social conception as a natural one. Conceiving the social world as a collection of independent individuals became possible in this period because, for the first time, society itself came to have that structure. The breakdown of feudal socioeconomic forms and relations and the rise of individual entrepreneurs, dependent on and responsible to themselves only, produced a society which corresponded much more closely to the atomistic picture than previous societies had. The conception of a collection of atomized individuals expressed well the life form of this new capitalist class, for whom the old, feudal state forms and relations appeared as holistic entities imposed antagonistically on the pattern of their individual activities.

But as Hobbes saw it, individualism at its heart is really a very general kind of explanatory frame, much more general than simply a social or political doctrine. It is a deep methodological principle, from which economic individualism or political individualism emerges as a special case. What these individualisms have in common is their form: that there is an upper level possibility-space which "is" the sum of a set of individual possibility-spaces each with its own individual dynamic.

The general question I want to raise about such reductions is as follows. Is the overall possibility-space really just the sum of N copies of an individual space? Or are there, on the other hand, hidden presuppositions of a structural nature? We had a brief introduction to such structural presuppositions in chapter 1, in the case of the class which was graded on a curve. A criterion emerged from that example for telling whether structural presuppositions were at work.

The essence of the criterion is to see what combinations of individual possibilities are jointly possible. If any combination of individual possibilities *is* jointly possible, we have a true case of reducibility. But in the typical case these generalized counterfactual conditionals (e.g., what if everyone had property P?) fail, and then we may infer that there are hidden structural presuppositions. In such cases a simpleminded atomism will fail, and we will have to focus on the structural presuppositions which are making the explanation possible.

This basic strategy is the foundation for what I will be doing in the rest of this work. I will be looking at a variety of examples of individualism in social theory and finding in each case hidden structural presuppositions. The nature of those presuppositions rules out the reductionist program in social theory.

But before going on to talk about social theory, I want first to discuss a case of "individualism" in natural science, one which is often held up as a paradigm for social individualism: the case of the reduction of the thermodynamics of gases to the statistical mechanics of the molecules which comprise it. This example is interesting in its own right but also as an example of certain anti-individualist principles that I will be using later on.

It was hailed as a great victory of mechanist reductionism when Boltzmann and others succeeded in deriving the laws governing the global properties of gases (temperature, pressure, volume) from a set of assumptions that amounted to postulating that the gas consisted of a large number of individual Newtonian molecules.

I think that the philosophical significance of this reduction has been misunderstood and that, when examined in detail, it does not support the kinds of claims that philosophers have made on its behalf. Here I want to look at that reduction as a paradigm for individualism, to see what kind of individualism it really is.

The gas is presented to us globally as an extended substance with various macroproperties: pressure, volume, and temperature. The most important law on this macrolevel is the Boyle–Charles law:

$$PV = kT,$$

where P is the pressure of the gas, V is the volume, and T is the temperature (k is a constant).

For the microlevel assume first that the gas is composed of tiny, hard, independent molecules; these are the "individuals." Assume further that these molecules collide with one another and with the walls of the box in a way describable by standard Newtonian mechanics. This is the microlevel. We will also need some connecting principles ("bridge laws") which enable us to identify P, V, and T with constructs on the microlevel. (For example, T is identified with the average kinetic energy of the gas molecules.) Having done all this, we can derive the Boyle–Charles law from the statistical theory of the behavior of the ensemble of molecules.

But there are some complications in this derivation that are important for our purposes. So let us consider it in detail, following a classic source, Nagel's *Structure of Science*. Nagel proceeds by postulating a microlevel of tiny Newtonian molecules and observes:

A further assumption must be introduced . . . that the probability of a molecule's occupying an assigned phase cell is the same for all molecules and is equal to the probability of a molecule's occupying any other phase cell and (subject to certain qualifications involving among other things the total energy of the system) the probability that one molecule occupies a phase cell is independent of the occupation of that cell by any other molecule.[19]

Let us set out carefully Nagel's independence assumptions. The key concept is that of a phase cell, a region in the state-space of a molecule, the product of a location interval with a velocity interval. Thus at every point in time every molecule is in one phase cell or another. If we represent such a phase cell by (X, V), Nagel's independence assumptions can be put this way:

1. For all molecules a, b, and all intervals (X, V), probability $[a\epsilon\,(X,\,V)]$ = probability $[b\epsilon\,(X,\,V)]$.

This assumption is unobjectionable; it postulates a homogeneity among the molecules. The others are:

2. For all molecules a, and intervals (X, V), (X', V'), probability $[a\epsilon\,(X,\,V)]$ = probability $[a\epsilon\,(X',\,V')]$.
3. For all molecules a, b, and intervals (X, V), probability $[b\epsilon\,(X,\,V)]$ is independent of the probability $[a\epsilon\,(X,\,V)]$.

Both of these are false. They are invalidated by those things that Nagel refers to as "certain qualifications involving among other things the total energy of the system." Let us see what those "qualifications" are.

First and foremost is *conservation of energy*. Obviously, energy must be conserved in all transactions affecting the gas or else PV could decrease relative to T if, for example, heat energy were allowed to dissipate. So energy must be conserved. But the total energy of the gas is the sum of the kinetic energies of the particles:

$$E = \tfrac{1}{2}\,(m_1 v_1{}^2 + \ldots + m_n v_n{}^2).$$

Assuming for convenience that all the masses have value 1, we get

$$(v_1{}^2 + \ldots + v_n{}^2) = \text{constant}.$$

This flatly contradicts assumption 3 above because you cannot say,

19. E. Nagel, *The Structure of Science* (New York: Harcourt Brace, 1961), p. 344.

"Pick *n* numbers at random, independently, but the sum of their squares must be a given constant." The overall requirement of conservation of energy, then, violates the independence of the "individuals," the molecules of the gas.

Assumption 2 is also false (even if we add the requirement that the intervals be the same size), for it is violated by the standard assumption of a normal distribution of velocities.

The failure of these independence assumptions tells us that we do not really have a case of a global property arising as a simple aggregate of independent individuals. There is, to be sure, a collection of individuals (the gas molecules) with an individual nature given by Newtonian mechanics, according to which they are essentially small elastic particles. But the properties of the gas, like the Boyle–Charles law, do not arise simply from this individual nature. We must make, in addition, strong assumptions about the *collective* possibilities of the system, assumptions which are imposed on the individual nature and do not in any sense follow from it. Their effect is exactly like the effect of the kinematical conditions discussed earlier: to restrict sharply the a priori possibilities of the system.

Because the effect of such additional assumptions is a reduction of the dimensions of the problem (a reduction in the degrees of freedom), we may expect that explanations taking place in the presence of such assumptions can take a greatly simplified form. In the foxes and rabbits example, the local equations were also of huge dimension. But we knew that on the global level all that is relevant to the level of the two populations are their previous levels. There the imposed kinematical condition tells us in effect: forget about the individual foxes and rabbits; especially, forget about differences among them; they are all irrelevant. Any state in which there are N foxes and M rabbits is "the same" as any other.[20]

Here too the passage to the statistical point of view, renouncing the possibility of explaining individual differences among the molecules, is the result of these imposed structural presuppositions.

In each case the test that brought out the nontrivial sociology was the formation of a generalized contrary-to-fact conditional, posed as a question:

20. Well, *almost* any. We typically neglect statistically freakish distributions (e.g., all the foxes in one corner) which would invalidate the law. We suppose Maxwell's demon not to be at work.

If the rabbit had not been at x, t, would it have avoided being eaten?

Could everyone in the class have gotten an A?

Could all the molecules have velocity v?

In each case the answer is no. Generalizing this, we can formulate the principle: *Whenever a global property is not simply a sum of* N *individual properties (a fact revealed by the test above), the explanation of that global property will involve structural presuppositions.*

This idea, that the reduction of thermodynamics is not really to an "individualistic" level, is not widely recognized; in fact, I have been able to find it in only one treatment, A. I. Khinchin's excellent *Mathematical Foundations of Statistical Mechanics*. He develops there the notion of something's being a *component* of a mechanical system, which corresponds basically to what we have been calling an "individual." Suppose $E(x_1, \ldots, xn)$ is the total energy of a system, and suppose further that E can be represented "as a sum of two terms E_1 and E_2, where the first term depends on some (not all) of the dynamical coordinates, and the second term depends on the remaining coordinates" (p. 38). We can therefore write $E = E_1 + E_2$, where

$$E_1 = E_1 (x_1, \ldots, x_k),$$
$$E_2 = E_2 (x_{k+1}, \ldots, x_n).$$

"In such a case we agree to say that the set . . . of the dynamical coordinates of the given system is decomposed into two components."

In other words, in such a case we have the global property "energy" expressible as the sum of two independent individual properties, the energies of the two components. Now it is natural to think, reductionistically, that the molecules of the gas are its components in this sense, that is, that the total energy of the gas is the sum of the independent energies of the molecules. But there is a paradox here. Although this presentation assumes the independence of the energies of the particles, the assumptions of conservation of energy and the normal distribution of velocities absolutely require that the particles interact energetically! Khinchin writes:

> The statistical mechanics bases its method precisely on a possibility of such an exchange of energy between various particles constituting the matter. However, if we take the particles constituting the given physical system to be its components in the above defined sense [i.e., the individuals],

we are excluding the possibility of any energetical interaction between them. Indeed, if the Hamiltonian function, which expresses the energy of our system, is a sum of functions each depending only on the dynamic coordinates of a single particle (and representing the Hamiltonian function of this particle), then, clearly, the whole system of equations [describing the overall dynamics of the system] splits into component systems each of which describes the motion of some separate particle and is not connected in any way with other particles. Hence the energy of each particle, which is expressed by its Hamiltonian function, appears as an integral of equations of motion, and therefore remains constant.[21]

In other words, because the sum of the energies is constant, if the particles really were independent, the individual energies would have to be constant too! But this is absurd, and so we must deny the fact that the total energy is simply the sum of the N independent individual energies. He continues immediately:

The serious difficulty so created is resolved by the fact that we can consider particles of matter as only approximately isolated energetical components. There is no doubt that a precise expression for the energy of the system must contain also terms which depend simultaneously on the energy of several particles, and which assure the possibility of an energetical interaction between the particles (from a mathematical point of view, prevent the splitting of the system into systems referring to single particles).[22]

What Khinchin is saying here is what I am claiming about such individualisms in general. The "individuals" are not really separable (they are "only approximately isolated") and structural presuppositions are at work, so that the real microlevel consists of a set of individuals together with a nontrivial sociology.

The interaction effects, which are *quantitatively* negligible for the Boyle–Charles law, are nevertheless qualitatively important for understanding it. Moreover, as the gas begins to get highly compressed, these interaction effects become significant even quantitatively, and the Boyle–Charles law no longer holds. Thus, changes in certain parameters can change the structural conditions.

•   •   •

21. A. I. Khinchin, *The Mathematical Foundations of Statistical Mechanics*, trans. G. Gamow (New York: Dover, 1949), p. 18.
22. Ibid.

The point of this discussion has been to examine atomistic reductionism in the theory of gases. I want now to turn to the primary focus of this work: social theories.

3 Individualism in Social Thought

Economic Individualism

The point of the gas example was to show how a certain individualistic reduction had structural presuppositions. As we turn to individualism in social theory the general claim is the same. Behind any would-be individualism, there are structural presuppositions at work.

The first problem I want to study is the problem of economic justice: How are the products of society distributed among people? This problem, so-called distributive justice, is often thought to be *the* question of social justice. This is a mistake. At the very least, there are a number of other significant factors—the nature and extent of political freedom, the forms and types of social and cultural institutions, and the kind of individual that the society fosters. There is even some reason to think that certain aspects, especially questions of democracy, are more important to the justice of society than the economic factors.

Nevertheless, my focus in this chapter will be exclusively on the economic aspects of justice. In doing so, I am probably contributing to the unfortunate tendency to ignore the other aspects and talk only about economics. Much of the recent discussion of social justice has suffered from this one-sidedness, and although I want to talk about economics here, it should not be assumed that that is the only subject worth talking about.

The standard way to ask the question about economic justice is to ask for the justification of the economic distribution in the form of the question Why do individuals receive the economic shares which they do? This may sound like a straightforward statement of the problem, but in fact it involves several significant presuppositions.

The first concerns what kind of "why?" question it is. What are we asking when we ask why individuals receive the shares that they do? On the one hand we are asking for a *justification,* a reason for thinking that it is right or good that people receive those shares, or a condemnation, a reason for thinking it bad or wrong. On the other hand we are also asking for an *explanation,* an account of how those shares came to be. The relation between these two types of endeavor is very complex.

There is clearly a logical distinction to be drawn between explanation and justification. If I show up an hour late for an appointment with you, I could conceivably explain why I did it without justifying the act ("I forgot") or attempt to justify it without explaining why I did it ("You do this all the time"). Typically, though, I will try to do both and justify my act by way of an explanation.[1]

All these possibilities exist with regard to the question of the economic distribution. We may explain it while leaving open the question of justification, e.g., by correlating economic status with something like "years of schooling." On the other hand we can seek to justify it without asking for its explanation, as someone would be doing who said, "Economic inequality is good. It gives you something to aspire to." But again, typically, we do the two together, the one by way of the other.

Having distinguished these two modes, I will often conflate them. This follows ordinary usage, which tends to use the word *explanation* indifferently for the two functions. When I show up late for the appointment, you look at me and say, "You'd better have an explanation," but what you really mean is not that (for of course there is an explanation). You mean, "You'd better have an explanation of a certain kind, one which justifies (or excuses) your act."

The situation is the same in social philosophy. Typically, justifications or criticisms of the economic distribution proceed via explanations of it. Examples include justifications of economic inequality which explain it as the result of market forces, biological needs, or hard work or as a "meritocracy"; each of these proceeds via a causal explanation of the inequality. On the other hand are critiques of inequality which condemn it by explaining that it is caused by exploitation, racial discrimination, or the need for "conspicuous consumption." In each of these cases, what is basic is a certain explanation (different in each case) of why individuals have the shares that they do.

1. There are still other possibilities: I may, for example, try to *excuse* the act. If I say "I was tied up in traffic," this is an excuse, not a justification. Excuses will not concern us here, but see J. L. Austin, "A Plea for Excuses," in *Philosophical Papers,* ed. J. O. Urmson and G. J. Warnock (Oxford: Clarendon Press, 1961).

It is instructive to note that this is a quite particular formulation of the question of economic justice, with its own presuppositions. It presupposes that the question of economic justice reduces to the problem of explaining facts about individuals. The basic object of explanation is

why A has P,

where P stands for A's share, and the problem of explaining the social distribution then becomes the problem of explaining why

A_1 has P_1
A_2 has P_2
.
.
.
A_n has P_n.

Framing the object in this way gives a certain slant to the question and limits the kinds of things we can ask. We cannot, for example, ask for the explanation of patterns or overall properties of the distribution. We cannot simply ask why there is inequality. All we can ask about is why (or how) individuals come to have the properties which they do. Thus the question is posed in a specifically particulatized way. What is explained are occasions of individual people coming to have certain properties.

Such a view insists that the question of explaining one person's share is logically independent of explaining anyone else's share. Even using the word *share* is not right, for it connotes some larger totality of which the individuals are merely parts. It is better to speak of individual *holdings*.[2]

My purpose in this chapter is to examine a family of economic explanations in which the object of explanation is construed in this way.

Theories of the Market
One basic kind of answer to the question of the distribution of in-

2. The term *individual holdings* and the associated way of posing the question of economic distribution are from Nozick's *Anarchy, State and Utopia,* the clearest contemporary statement of classical economic individualism. I shall draw on Nozick's formulations throughout the discussion of the nature of markets. My criticisms, however, are of the market not of Nozick's formulations of it.

dividual holdings explains those holdings as the result of the differential
rewards which a free market bestows on its various competitors. The
essence of such theories of the market is the picture c f a collection of
individuals freely trading among themselves and producing thereby a
distribution of returns that vary from individual to individual. The object
of such explanations is the set of individual outcomes or holdings, and
the form of the explanation it gives is that they are the result of the
free bargaining and trading, that is, the free choices, of the entrepreneurs who constitute the market.

The historical source of this conception, and the first clear formulation of it, was Adam Smith's *Wealth of Nations.* We can recognize in it
a basic form of atomism: the idea that overall social forms can be explained as the aggregate result of the interaction of a number of independent individuals, each with a pregiven individual nature. The atoms in
Smith's model are the individual entrepreneurs, each with a natural
"propensity to truck and barter."

This conception of the market has been used to explain and thereby justify the distribution of holdings in two distinct ways: justifications
which focus on individual rights, on the one hand, and, on the other,
justifications which focus on the desirable overall consequences of the
operation of such a market. Both types of justification are important.
The individual rights justification is based on the observation that we can
justify a state of affairs by showing that it arose as a result of the free
choices of the individuals involved in it. Such a situation was not imposed on the individuals; they chose it. The consequentialist justification, on the other hand, turns on delivering the goods. Smith argued
that if such a market were left to its own devices, the self-interest of the
traders would result in a highly desirable overall pattern. The laws of
supply and demand would set prices fairly, the goods produced and sold
would be the ones people wanted to buy, and the competition of the
market would force the entrepreneurs to improve continually the nature
of their products. All this would happen because there is competition.
The operation of the market thus produces an overall situation which is
in many respects optimal. Smith marveled at this "invisible hand," which
directed the entrepreneurs, each concerned only with personal gain, to
do the thing that was ultimately most conducive to the public good.[3]

---

3. Contemporary economics has taken over these optimality results as "invisible
hand theorems." Their structure parallels Leibniz's argument that this is the best

But not only does the operation of the market produce the best possible product mix, it also rewards the worthy entrepreneur. The return to entrepreneurs is directly proportional to their success in meeting consumer demand. Therefore, the differences in individual returns can be justified as differential rewards for having produced what society (i.e., individual people) wanted.

This gives us the second basic type of justification of the distribution of holdings: a free market delivers the goods (to those who earn it by their contributions). Taken together, these two kinds of justification serve as the fundamental theoretical underpinnings of capitalist economics. The two virtues are theoretically separable: the system which least violated individual rights would not necessarily have to be the one which best delivered the goods, and the reverse would not be necessarily true. But they *are* both true of the capitalist system, this theory claims, and therein lies its genius.

My intention here is to provide a critique of those underpinnings and of the economic concept of the market. Much of it is not really new. Much of it is derived from Marx, with additions from contemporary Marxists like Joan Robinson. I take the trouble at this point to present a Marxist critique of the economic theory of the market for several reasons: first, in spite of the time that has passed since its outlines were first laid down, a large number of people are completely unaware of it. Second, much of it is still valid. Third, it can be hard to find in the classical texts. I am presenting it here because its basic structure fits well with what I have been saying about explanatory frames in general and about individualistic explanations in particular. So the analytic tools I have been developing turn out to give a natural expression for this critique, making it a kind of elementary economics from an advanced point of view.[4]

---

of all possible worlds because God has both the desire and the ability to create it. Entrepreneurs have the desire and ability to satisfy consumer demand, hence the market produces the best of all possible product mixes.

4. Such a critique would also be timely. The past few years have seen a tremendous resurgence in talk about the free market. Market libertarians are on the offensive in various areas of theory, and promarket thinking is even trickling down to newspapers and magazines, with some help from the advertising budgets of some of our larger corporations. A public relations campaign has been launched on behalf of the market. Educational materials prepared by corporate interests are being

Markets and Individual Rights

Let us begin our discussion of the market with the sort of justification which stresses the individual rights of the participants. This is the point that Nozick's book rests on. From the point of view of individual rights the most important fact about the market is that it is *free* in the sense that people participate in it voluntarily. Consequently, whatever holdings come about as a result of such activities have at least this much to be said for them, that they arose with the consent of the people concerned. This gives us a simple pattern of justification for holdings. Show that the holdings came about voluntarily, and you have shown that they violate no one's rights.

The basic fact about a market is that a person's holdings at a given time are the accumulated result of the person's trades. This provides us with a style of justification: a holding is justified if it was the result of a free trade. But of course we cannot simply say that a holding is legitimate if it was acquired in a free trade, for this involves a regress, as Nozick recognizes. For when we said, "The holding is the product of free trades," we must add, "trades, that is, from the *previous* state." And so the question arises, Where did the item traded come from? How did the trader acquire *it*? From another trade? Clearly, this regress of justification must end at a point where things traded are acquired de novo. The justification of holdings combines these two types of justification, which in Nozick's terms are a theory of justice in the appropriation of unheld things and a theory of justice in transfer. A holding will then be just if it was acquired by means which do not violate the two principles.

Let us examine these two principles more closely, beginning with the principle of justice in the appropriation of unheld things. This principle is supplied by the theory of property acquisition of Locke's *Second Treatise of Civil Government*. Locke considers people in a "state of nature," that is,

> a state of perfect freedom to order their actions and dispose of their possessions and persons as they see fit, within the bounds of the law of nature, without depending on the will of any other man.

He asks, in effect, what might entitle someone in that state to appropriate some unheld thing? His answer is:

---

distributed in the schools, and professorships of "free enterprise" are being endowed at universities.

> The *labor* of his body and the work of his hands, we may say, are
> properly his. Whatsoever, then, he removes out of the state that nature
> hath provided and left it in, he hath mixed his labor with it, and joined
> it to something which is his own, and thereby makes it his property.[5]

Here we have a simple theory of entitlements. Someone who "mixes
his labor" with an unheld thing is entitled to it. This provides the
foundation, the base step, of the historical entitlement process. Look
at the original acquisitions and see how they were acquired.

How well does this theory work? Well enough in a certain class of
cases. It works well in the state of nature, for example, and in real situations which resemble the state of nature in a crucial way: that individual
destinies are *independent* in the sense that someone's becoming entitled
to something, say a piece of land, does not seriously affect other people.
Locke recognizes the need for this assumption and requires that the
appropriation of an unheld thing by someone be subject to the proviso
that there be "as much and as good left in common for others."
(Nozick calls this "the Lockean proviso.")

In cases where this Lockean proviso is satisfied, the theory of acquisition seems to meet our intuitive conceptions of just entitlement.
Locke's own example is "America in 1690": a pioneer settler cleared
a piece of land in the vast wilderness, cultivated it, improved it, and
otherwise "mixed his labor" with it. We would recognize a just claim
which that settler had to that piece of land and would dismiss someone else's claim to that land by pointing out that the settler did not
deprive anyone by that appropriation. We would say to the would-be
challenger, Go establish your own entitlement.

There will, however, be enormous problems in situations which violate
the Lockean proviso. If someone's appropriation of something ends
up depriving others in any way, the theory collapses and has nothing to
say about possible entitlements. In the language of the last chapter
there must be no kinematical conditions, no structural presuppositions,
no internal relations among individuals; they must be independent. If
this fails, that is, if someone's appropriation does not leave "as much
and as good" for others, the theory does not apply. This will be the
case in situations of scarce resources, as well as generally competitive
situations.

5. J. Locke, *Two Treatises of Government*, 2nd ed., ed. P. Laslett (Cambridge:
Cambridge University Press, 1967), p. 4.

Rousseau thought that this was the typical case. His view was in a way the opposite of Locke's. He saw society as having a collective entitlement to the things of nature, and an individual's appropriation of a thing as the denial of our collective access to it.

Rousseau therefore rejects the claims of would-be Lockean entitlement:

> In vain might they say: But I built this wall, I earned this field by my labor.

His reply is:

> By virtue of what do you presume to be paid at our expense for work we did not impose on you?[6]

Here we see two very deeply opposed pictures. In Rousseau's view, because the appropriation affects all of us, we collectively have a say in whether it is in our collective interest to grant the entitlement. On the other hand, for Locke, the independence of individuals allows for individual entitlement. The key to the situation is the Lockean proviso: Does the entitlement leave us much and as good for others? How we go about answering the question of whether the Lockean proviso is satisfied makes a crucial difference for the theory.

Let us turn our attention to the example of the distribution of holdings in the United States today. To answer the question of justification we would ultimately have to ask how the original acquisitions were made.

And so the question becomes how, in fact, those original acquisitions were made. In order to answer this, we must look at the histories of the great fortunes of Europe and America. There is a curious gap in Nozick's account in this regard, for he does not even attempt to apply his theory to justify any existing holdings. He insists, quite rightly, that the justice of a holding lies in the actual history which generated it. It is surprising that, having said this, he proceeds to say absolutely nothing about this actual history in any actual case. If we look at this history, we can see why. There is not a shred of hope of applying this original entitlement scheme in any real case.

Balzac once wrote: "Every great fortune begins with a crime," and

6. J. J. Rousseau, *Discourse on the Origin of Inequality,* ed. R. D. Masters (New York: St. Martin's Press, 1964), p. 31.

that is a much better summary of the nature of original acquisitions than Locke's.[7] Adam Smith called these original acquisitions "the primitive accumulation," and all of us have heard the stories about how they were made: hard work, ingenuity, deferment of gratification, thrift, "frugality, prudence, temperance and other industrial virtues" (William Graham Sumner). We have heard the parable about the squirrel and the nuts, and the one about the ant and the grasshopper. But "in actual history," Marx writes, "it is notorious that conquest, enslavement, robbery, murder, briefly, force play the great part."

This is certainly true of the primitive accumulations which began the fortunes of Europe and America. The land itself was certainly not "unheld,"[8] and although *some* annexations may have left as much and as good for the native inhabitants, the bulk of them surely did not. Consequently all appropriation of land in the Americas is under a cloud.

The situation with regard to natural resources is, if possible, even worse:

> The discovery of gold and silver in America, the extirpation, enslavement, and entombment in mines of the aboriginal population, the beginning of the conquest and looting of the East Indies, the turning of Africa into a warren for the commercial hunting of black skins, signalised the rosy dawn of the era of capitalist production. These idyllic proceedings are the chief momenta of primitive accumulation. In the tender annals of Political Economy, the idyllic reigns from time immemorial.[9]

Any good history tells the same story about the people who amassed the fortunes of the great families of the United States. John D. Rockefeller had competitors dynamited, Ford had striking workers shot. The crimes in the history of the great American fortunes rule out any possibility of employing a historical entitlement justification.

We must, therefore, forget about applying it to any actual distribution of holdings. But we also have some theoretical reasons for thinking that

7. The quotation from Balzac is used by Mario Puzo as the epigraph for *The Godfather*, a book which suggests, in effect, that the Mafia should be seen as a capitalist enterprise which must commit its crimes of accumulation in the glare of present scrutiny.

8. The very application of the *concept* of "holdings" is problematic in this case, for the native cultures in America did not contain concepts of private ownership of land. Was their land therefore "unheld"?

9. *Capital,* vol. 1, p. 714.

it cannot hold in typical situations. The Lockean proviso, requiring
that "as much and as good" be left for others, is almost never met.
Instead, structural conditions ensure that one individual's actions inevitably affect the welfare of others.

The foundation step of the justification process is therefore founder-
ing in difficulties, both theoretical and practical.

Let us pretend that these difficulties can be solved, that the original
acquisitions *can* be justified, so that we can pass to the discussion of the
ongoing process of market trades. The basic anatomy of the process is
familiar from elementary economics. You have corn, I have wheat; we
agree to exchange X amount of corn for Y amount of wheat. Taken
generally, this produces the market: a large number of small, roughly
equal entrepreneurs, freely engaging, in Nozick's phrase, in "capitalist
acts between consenting adults."

What is wrong with this picture? One curious fact is that in this
classic description of the working of the capitalist market, the concept
of *capital* appears nowhere. Everything is wheat and corn. But reality
is far from a homogeneous system of traders, each buying and selling
goods. There is a basic qualitative stratification in the system between
two kinds of traders: on the one hand, those who have capital and are
seeking to buy labor power and, on the other, those who have no
capital and therefore must sell their labor.

This structural difference introduces basic changes in the model. The
owner of capital makes an agreement with the worker, the wage bargain:
How much of the goods which the worker produces will be returned
as wages? The owner of capital is in competition with the worker over
the respective shares of the output.

Of course, in this bargaining the owner is in an enviable position because his ownership of capital gives him the ability to dictate the
terms of the agreement. The worker must make an agreement today in
order to eat, while the capital serves as a cushion that enables its owner
to press a harder bargain. Suddenly the Smithian picture of a system
of homogeneous traders metamorphoses into a very different picture,
on which one class of traders, the owners of capital, uses the bargaining
power which this gives them to drive a hard bargain against the others.
The coercive nature of this "agreement" therefore invalidates the "free
trade" style of justification, which rests on the fact that each individual
chooses freely to enter into the exchanges.

Capital, in this view, is not a sum of money or a machine but a certain social relation, and with it the power to command the resources of others. In other words the market contains a structural or an internal relation among the individual destinies. As in the examples of the previous chapters, like the grading-on-a-curve example, what looks like a property of an individual, "owning capital" (getting an A), is really a disguised relation among the individuals. The argument for this lies in the test question: Could everyone earn a living by owning capital? The answer is no. If everyone owned capital, everyone would be immune to the bargaining power of capital; hence the "free" nature of the wage bargain would break down.

The structural condition makes property into a relation, a power relation. This fact is not widely appreciated, and most people, including economists, continue to talk about property as a relation between a person and a thing not as a relation among people. Rousseau was perhaps the first to articulate this clearly. He remarks that property can be viewed in two ways. On the one hand, it is that which makes someone immune to the influence of others (one retreats defensively to one's little plot of land), but, on the other, it is something that gives one power to influence others. This distinction seems to have been lost in recent discussions of the subject.

The essence of this critique of the market lies in insisting on the structural relations that hold among individuals. The classical conception of the market sees individuals atomistically and therefore maintains that an individual's holding can be justified by looking only at that individual. This was the original appeal of the libertarian picture: that the validity of an agreement could be established by establishing A's willingness, B's willingness, and the fact that they are entitled to trade what they are trading. Justification could be carried out purely *locally*. But this is not the case. The Lockean proviso, which began as the background assumption, ends up dominating the question of the validity of the agreement. Every transfer becomes constrained, not just by the states of the parties to the transfer but by the state of everyone else too. In this way the essence of the libertarian picture has been lost; overall social welfare affects the validity of any particular exchange. The same thing is true in the case of ongoing trades. Whether or not A is being coerced into trading with B is a function, not just of the local properties of A and B, but of the overall distribution of holdings and the willingness of other traders to trade with A.

The difference between the atomist account and the structural account therefore lies in the relations among the individual destinies, for that affects the kinds of explanations we can make. If what we are trying to explain is really a relational property, the process of explaining it individual by individual simply will not work. And most if not all of the interesting properties in social explanation *are* inherently relational: for example, the properties of being rich or poor, employed or unemployed. One aspect of this was captured by Jencks et al. in their recent *Inequality:*

> The rich are not rich because they eat filet mignon or own yachts. Millions of people can now afford these luxuries, but they are not "rich" in the colloquial sense. *The rich are rich because they can afford to buy other people's time.* They can hire other people to make their beds, tend their gardens, and drive their cars. *These are not privileges that become more widely available as people become more affluent.*[10]

The internal relations make this case into an application of the machinery of chapters 1 and 2. If the term *rich* denotes what is actually a relational property (being able to command the time of others), we cannot truly answer the question (why is A rich?) by citing factors which are properties of the individual A. Just as in the grading example, there are strong structural presuppositions and those presuppositions make certain kinds of explanation impossible.

The structural conditions, in violating the independence required by the market model, are the main things separating radical or Marxist accounts of the economic system from other accounts. Other accounts, whether liberal or conservative, attempt to talk about the economic system without considering these interrelations. Conservative accounts, like Nozick's, have their source in the false belief that individuals really can be said to have individual historical justifications for their holdings. Liberal accounts are somewhat different. They typically attempt to talk about economic justification in the absence of any historical or causal assumptions at all.[11] For the liberal the problem of economic distribution is raised by a simple juxtaposition: some are poor while others are rich. These two states of affairs are compared, side by side, and then the utilitarian question of redistribution becomes relevant. We could say

10. (New York: Basic Books, 1972), p. 6 (emphasis added).
11. For a good example of these two positions with regard to the world hunger problem, see the contributions of Garrett Hardin and Peter Singer in W. Aiken and H. Lafollette, eds., *World Hunger and Moral Obligation* (Englewood Cliffs, N.J.: Prentice-Hall, 1977).

that the liberal critique of inequality is that some are poor while others are rich, but, by contrast, the radical critique is that some are poor *because* others are rich.

. . .

Two very different pictures, the Smith/Locke/Nozick, on the one hand, and the structural or Marxist on the other, both emerge from considering the anatomy of the market. In a way this is paradoxical since they are so diametrically opposed. How could two such pictures emerge of one and the same object? I think it is because the market itself has both aspects.

Specifically, in cases in which the degree of collusion among traders is negligible, where Lockean provisos are satisfied, and where there is an independence of individual destinies, the Smith model seems to work, both as economics and as an account of our ethical intuitions. But in cases which violate these independence assumptions, the Smith model is no longer valid. So it lends itself to this duality because under some circumstances it will really behave as its advocates promise, whereas in other circumstances it will act as Marx says.

This duality provides us with an interesting example of the relation between one theory and another that supersedes it. A theory which is a would-be replacement for another cannot simply contradict it and say no more; it must also give us some account of why the old one worked as well as it did. Typically, this will take the form of showing how the old theory worked in a limited class of cases of the world according to the new theory. The classic example of this is the relation between Newtonian and Einsteinian physics: the relativistic theory shows how the classical theory is approximately true for low velocities and large masses. The relativistic theory then goes beyond the classical by showing how the world diverges from the classical model as velocities get larger.

A similar statement can be made about the relation of Smithian and Marxian economics as theories of how capitalism works. Smithian economics works for small trades among small traders in a homogeneous system.[12]

---

12. Another example of this kind of correspondence principle, more analogous to the market case, is given by the ideal gas law. The Boyle–Charles law tells us that $PV = kT$, but this is only valid when the intermolecular distances are so large that the forces of attraction between molecules do not operate. When the gas is compressed into a sufficiently small volume the intermolecular forces, previously negligible, become significant. These interaction effects among the individual molecules give the gas an entirely different behavior.

We know, in general, that a system of equations may have a given form of solution or behavior in a given region of initial conditions, but, as the state passes out of that region, the form of the solution may change (e.g., the transition from liquid to gas).

Similarly, the Smithian transfers *are* justice preserving in a neighborhood of the homogeneous situation (that is to say, where holdings are roughly equal, Smithian transfers do preserve justice), but when the state (levels of holdings) passes out of that region, in particular when some people begin to have such holdings as to constitute *capital,* then the form of the solution changes, new dynamical forms appear (exploitation and so on), and the resulting solution will no longer be justice preserving.

This is another defect of Nozick's iterative model. It is absolutely essential to his construction that iterations of the just-transfer principle never take us outside the boundaries of justice. No matter how many times we apply the principle of justice in transfer, the results are still justified. He uses the analogy of proof in logic: no matter how many times we iterate rules of inference, what we have at the end is still a theorem. But the corresponding statement about transfers, that they can *never* result in a qualitatively different situation, just seems wrong. Smithian transfers preserve *approximate* justice, which is a notion like "near." The result of a small number of transfers will leave you "near" the original, but the result of a lot of transfers may not.

The Object of Market Explanations

In Nozick's presentation of the market, the object of explanation is the holding of a particular individual at a particular time. This is important. In fact it is crucial to his whole presentation, for the justification of a holding lies in the particular history which produced it. He recognizes the importance of this object and defends it explicitly:

> Suppose there are separate entitlement explanations showing the legitimacy of my having my holdings and your having yours, and the following question is asked: Why is it legitimate that I hold what I do *and* you hold what you do: why is that joint fact *and all the relations contained within it* legitimate? If the conjunction of the two separate explanations will not be held to explain in a unified manner the joint fact . . . then some patterned principle would appear to be necessary. (p. 200)

It is "patterned principles" that Nozick wants to avoid. In order to avoid them he rejects those "unified explanations" and states in their place a general principle of scientific explanation:

> With scientific explanation of particular facts the usual practice is to consider some conjunctions of explained facts as not requiring separate explanations, but as being explained by the conjunctions of the explanations of the conjuncts. (If E_1 explains e_1 and E_2 explains e_2, then $E_1 \wedge E_2$ explains $e_1 \wedge e_2$.) (p. 220)

Each separate holding is explained separately; by definition there are no connections. People who do not view explanation in this atomistic way, he says, see the world as it "looks to paranoid persons,"[13] or "persons having certain sorts of dope experiences."

Let us leave aside questions about his dope epistemology and concentrate on this claim purely as a principle about explanation. We can see how much work it is doing here. Most obviously, it forces the discussion of justice to be a discussion solely about the holdings of individuals. This is, to say the least, restrictive: there are questions about how desirable, how just, a society is, questions which are larger than that. There are, for example, questions about *collective* goods, goods which are not privately held but publicly provided: parks or schools or less tangible things like the social or cultural climate. Nozick's object does not allow such issues to be discussed. Further it does not allow us to discuss any of the facts about a society which cannot be expressed as a single individual's holdings. As we saw, there are many examples of such internal relations. Being rich or poor, being employed or unemployed, and being the victim of racial injustice are only the most prominent examples. The causal chain that produces any of these states is a chain which leads back through the overall structure of the system.

Nozick's atomism is even more questionable as a general philosophy of explanation. There is a clear sense in which the demand for an explanation can be rightly addressed to a conjunction of facts. Sometimes, what we want is an explanation of a conjunction not a conjunction of separate explanations. If a child asks, Why do boys become doctors and girls become nurses? a certain contrast has caught the child's attention. The question the child is asking cannot be answered by saying: "First, let me tell you why boys become doctors; they become doctors because that is a rewarding, well-paying job. Now I will tell you why girls become nurses; because it gives them a chance to help people." It is the contrast which demands explanation.

---

13. Pynchon notes: "The first law of paranoia, everything is connected to everything else." Of course, his point is that everything *is* connected to everything else.

In fact, in chapter 1 we saw that in a way every explanation is of a contrast. In the grading example the explanation for the overall distribution of grades was precisely not the conjunction of the fifty separate explanations:

why Mary got an A
.
.
.
why Harold got a C.

Instead, there was an overall pattern (the distribution of grades) that was capable of being explained in a unified way. Similarly, in the case of the gas the overall pattern, that there is a normal distribution of velocities, is capable of being explained, and the explanation is not the conjunction of the separate explanations of the velocities of the individual molecules. Indeed, there were no nontrivial explanations of those molecular facts.

There are patterns which must be explained as patterns: their explanations "seek their own level." Such patterns in a society are obviously relevant to our assessment of that society. At least one aspect of the question of the justice of a distribution lies in its patterns and in the *principles* of distribution (conscious or unconscious) which explain those patterns. Suppose, for example, that in a particular kind of market system structural facts ensured that 40 percent of the population would be impoverished at any given time. Or suppose, as in the foxes and rabbits case, that structural factors ensured that levels of holdings went through large cycles. Is that not relevant to the assessment of that system?

Nozick's object of explanation suffers from *hyperconcreteness.* The trouble, as in the foxes and rabbits case, is that the object of explanation is too specific. We do not really want to know why that rabbit was in that exact place, and we do not want to know why that very person has that level of holdings. We would really like to know what *stabilities* the outcome has. Suppose the initial distribution of holdings was perturbed from its actual state? Are there general states of affairs which would have been the case even for the altered initial conditions? If there are, we want to know this. Letting explanation seek its own level, we want some account of those general facts.

The market frame, as Nozick employs it, cannot answer such questions, because it is designed to explain only particular holdings. It avoids the question of whether such explanations are stable in neighborhoods of those levels. If we explain the holding of A at some time by citing earlier holdings and subsequent trades, we have no idea what would have been the case had the situation been otherwise. The hyperspecific object does not answer this kind of question. In the foxes and rabbits case, what made such an object unsuitable was the fact that there were "redundant causalities." This meant that given a certain high level of foxes, we could explain why 80 percent of the rabbits were eaten, an explanation that differed fundamentally from considering the 80 percent who were eaten and asking of each why *it* was eaten. The pattern emerged at a higher level of explanation and therefore had to be explained at that level. The individualistic explanation, which took each of the rabbits, explained why it was eaten, and then conjoined those explanations, suffered from the fact that it made the 80 percent death rate look accidental, as if to say: had those rabbits not run into bad luck. . . . But in fact, given the fox level and the structural factors relating the two levels, 80 percent of the rabbits had to be eaten.

There are similar sorts of facts about the distribution of holdings, but an insistence on a hyperconcrete object of explanation prevents us from asking the questions.[14]

These facts about the explanation of patterns as opposed to the explanation of particular facts may help explain a paradoxical and puzzling conclusion which Jencks et al. reach in their *Inequality*. They study the various answers that have been offered to explain why some people are economically successful, such as intelligence, education, and family background. They conclude that none of these really plays a strong causal role. Instead, they say, the variations in economic status among individuals are caused by nonsystematic factors: "varieties of competence . . . the ability to hit a ball thrown at high speed, the ability to type a letter quickly and accurately" (p. 227). These factors are more or less random, which is doubly true of their other major cause of success: luck!

---

14. This is one of the ways in which the approach of Rawls's *A Theory of Justice* (Cambridge: Harvard University Press, 1972) is deeper and more profound than the market conception. In Rawls's approach, what gets assessed are precisely the principles of allocation, and his constructions are designed to give us a way to assess various competing principles or patterns. But the market conception has decided, pretheoretically, that there is only one just pattern (the market) and that therefore the only question is whether a particular distribution of holdings was reached in accord with it. The critique of principles does not arise.

Income also depends on luck: chance acquaintances who steer you to
one line of work rather than another, the range of jobs that happen to
be available in a particular community when you are job-hunting . . . ,
and a hundred other unpredictable accidents. (p. 227)

Jencks has been ridiculed as saying that "nothing causes anything" and
as saying that inequality, unemployment, and so on are caused by random or mysterious factors. Surely, we think, there are some nonchaotic
factors. Are black people just not as lucky as whites? Do "varieties of
competence" suddenly decline during recessions? Of course not. There
are certainly structural factors responsible for these things. It is paradoxical to say that income distribution is explained by chaotic local accidents.

The paradox can be partly resolved by realizing that the answer Jencks
has produced, in effect, "random and mysterious causes," really *is* the
answer, the only answer, to the individualistic or particularistic question

   Why does A_0 have income I_0?

For however unacceptable that answer is as an answer to the structural
question

   Why is there a given distribution of income?

it is the best possible answer to the question

   Why, given a distribution of income, does *this* person occupy *this*
   place in it?

Therefore, it constitutes a reductio ad absurdum, showing the impossibility of that individualistic question.

It also constitutes a reductio of the whole hyperspecific explanatory
frame which Nozick advocates. Not only do we want explanations of
patterns rather than individual facts, but it turns out that the individual
facts, like the individual velocities in the gas, are unexplainable!

Do Markets Deliver the Goods? To Whom?
We said earlier that the justifications which have been offered for the
market fall into two categories: those which stress the individual rights
of the participants and those which stress the overall beneficial consequences. We have been dealing so far only with the first line of justification. The second kind cites certain facts about the operation of markets.
First, it is claimed, competition in the market ensures that prices are

driven to the lowest point and that the products offered are those which people desire. Second, there is a set of claims about the distribution of income produced by such a market. Roughly, they are that success in the market is the reward for having satisfied consumer demand. Therefore, income distributes to those who are productive.

I will not discuss the first set of claims, about prices and products. Our experience with power plants and Pintos, to name just two examples, suggests that products are less than ideal, and this experience is confirmed by the theoretical writings of economists like Galbraith, which undermine the claims of productive efficiency.[15] In each case the efficiency claim is refuted by the fact that the market does not satisfy crucial assumptions of the model. For example, the market is supposed to keep prices down by competition among producers. But when the number of producers is small and the firms themselves are large, these producers find it is more profitable if they collectively keep prices up than if they compete against one another. This was the case in the "oil boycott," in which the major oil companies simply found it profitable to act as a tacit cartel. Similar things can be said about the quality and kind of product produced.

My concern here is with the question of distribution of income: Who gets it, and in virtue of what? The market view is that reward is proportional to contribution. In contemporary economics this is fundamental. Consider what is called the *production function:*

$$O = f(L, C).$$

This function expresses output O as a function of inputs of labor, L, and capital, C. For L units of labor and C units of capital we can produce $O = f(L, C)$ units of output. The nature of the function f naturally varies from process to process. For example, if we were interested in ditchdigging, the production function would tell us how many feet O of ditch can be dug in L number of person-hours using C number of shovels. Now let us suppose we are in the ditchdigging business. We can imagine each day's output being given back as payment to L and C for their roles in production. So we have a certain amount of O to be used in hiring varying mixes of L and C. We could, for example, share it by hiring a hundred people and five shovels. The production function tells us that we

15. See, e.g., his *The New Industrial State.*

get a certain amount of ditch out of this mix, a relatively *low* amount. At the other extreme we could hire five people and a hundred shovels, although this would also produce a low output. Somewhere in the middle is the optimal strategy, the mix which produces the greatest output. The rational entrepreneur pegs the production strategy to this point.

This gives us a purely economic theory of the distribution of income. In the optimal operation of the market, how much is paid back to *L* and *C* is purely a function of how profitably they contribute to production.

In a series of articles Joan Robinson has detailed the fallacies contained in this theory of distribution.[16] The basic point is this. Imagine we are at the end of the day and are about to pay labor and capital their respective shares. Each will be rewarded in proportion to the amount used. For labor, the amount contributed is measured easily, in person-hours (number of people $\times$ hours worked). But how can we measure how much capital we have used? What is the measure of the amount of capital? Robinson observes that behind this deceptively routine question of measurement index lies a very deep problem. We could, for example, measure the amount of capital by weighing it and pay it on the basis of how many pounds of machinery and so forth have been used. But that is obviously silly. How much the capital weighs is clearly irrelevant. It is better, we think, to measure it in dollars and pay it on the basis of the *worth* of the capital. But what is a given piece of capital worth? There's the rub. How much a given piece of capital is worth is a function of how profitable it is. But how profitable it is, is just how much of the output gets paid to it. In other words there is a circularity: to justify the rate of profit (the return to capital) we have introduced the notion of the value of the capital, but the value of a piece of capital is in turn a function of how much profit you can make by employing it. The value of the capital contained in a buggy whip factory declined sharply when the automobile became popular. And similarly, the value of a piece of capital in an area in which labor is highly organized is worth less than the same capital in an area in which labor is less highly organized.

16. See R. Harcourt, ed., *Readings in Capital Theory* (London: Penguin, 1973), and E. Nell, "Economics: The Rediscovery of Political Economy," in R. Blackburn, ed., *Ideology in Social Science* (New York: Vintage Books, 1977).

Consequently, the rate of profit cannot be explained as arising from purely economic factors. In fact it is determined by factors external to economics. Political factors, levels of unionization, and other such elements are the primary factors explaining the rate of profit. The rate of profit is higher in South Korea because the government does not allow unions. The rate of profit on capital in the production of home recording equipment has been made higher by court decisions holding that using such equipment to record commercial broadcasts does not violate copyright laws.

The profitability (and hence the "worth") of the one factor cannot be defined without the other. This failure of independence undercuts the attempt to show that the smooth functioning of the market allocates a return to each participant which is somehow proportional to that individual's "contribution." For we wanted a notion of the individual's *contribution,* but no clear sense can be given to the notion of the proportional contribution that one person makes to a collective effort.

A Structural Explanation of the Distribution of Income

We have seen a series of failures to explain the distribution of income. What they have in common is that they are all, in a way, too individualistic. They presuppose that the thing to be explained is a particular individual's holding and that all explanations can be built up as a logical sum of such atomic explanations. This hyperconcreteness was the real source of Jencks's paradox: that the distribution of income, construed as a question about individuals, has no nontrivial answer. ("Income depends on luck.") The interpretation I suggested was that Jencks's paradox be construed as a reductio of that question. If we look at the particular history which led to an individual's economic holding, we find that it is typically unstable: small perturbations would have qualitatively changed it. Such chaos precludes individualistic explanation. But there *are* overall patterns, and those overall patterns are capable of explanation on their own level. The situation is therefore parallel to the example of the gas. If we look at any particular molecule m_0, and ask

Why does m_0 have velocity v_0?

there is no nontrivial explanation. Each particle has an unstable local history. But the fact that there are no stable explanations of individual velocities does not mean that there are no stable explanations of *patterns* of distribution. There is, for example, a nontrivial explanation for why the distribution forms a normal curve; we explain this pattern as arising from interaction effects among the molecules, precisely what the atomistic model assumes nonexistent.

I would like to propose an analogous strategy in the explanation of patterns of income. We start with a shift in the object of explanation. We seek to explain the return not to an individual, Phil or Harriet, but to a social position occupied by an individual. A social position, like doctor or farmworker, is a structural property; it is defined relative to the other social positions. We can think of it as a point in a social geometry. Once we take the focus off the individual and place it on the social position, it becomes possible to give nontrivial explanations for why some kinds of positions are better rewarded than others. Since a position is essentially a point in the social geometry, the general form of the explanation of the return to a position is to look at the relations between that position and the other positions which constitute the structure.

In the atomistic model of the market, each agreement is reached in logical independence from every other. There are, in particular, no *coalitions.* The possibility of coalition radically alters the market. Cartels, monopolies, price-fixing agreements, and similar arrangements change the nature of the bargaining and divert a larger share of the distribution toward the coalition. This is especially true of price-fixing coalitions in the labor market, that is to say, labor unions. Such coalitions drive the bargain level above where it would be if each labor seller bargained independently.

This suggests a very general model: what is explained is the return to a particular social position (job type, location and so on) and the form of explanation is that *the return to a social position is explained by the degree of coalition surrounding that position.* The level of income at a position is explained by the level of unionization that obtains at that position.

There seems to be some intuitive evidence for this proposition. If one position is rewarded differently from another, the explanation lies not in characteristics of the individuals but in terms of the relative degree of coalition that exists at the two positions. For example:

Supermarket clerks, stockers, and checkers typically earn $5–9/hour.

On the other hand, clerk employees at fast-food franchises like McDonalds are paid very little, the legal minimum or less. What accounts for the difference? There is not that much difference between the type of job that the two do, certainly not enough to explain the difference in incomes. The real explanation seems to be that the supermarket clerks have a strong union and the fast-food employees have none at all.

In general, wherever there are strong unions or coalitions, they drive their income up. This is as true of the AMA as it is of the UAW. If mine workers are relatively better paid than farmworkers, we should seek the explanation in the fact that miners have organized to a higher degree than farmworkers. This in turn has a nontrivial explanation in terms of the basic structure of the job and particular historical factors. It was relatively easy to organize mine workers because of the conditions of their work. Mine work is fixed in one place and has a long-term work force that works cooperatively and lives near the mine and one another. Farmworkers, on the other hand, have transitory jobs and must constantly move from place to place, dissolving the natural ties that form the basis for coalitions.

People who write commercial jingles for big national advertising campaigns get paid surprisingly little, about $3,000–5,000 for a major jingle. On the other hand the artists who perform that jingle for the commercial will receive much more for their role. In any standard view this is paradoxical. Writing a song is much more difficult and requires a rarer talent than merely performing one, yet it is paid less. The only plausible explanation is that, by the sporadic nature of their work, jingle writers are not well organized and hence cannot drive an effective bargain with their employers. The musicians, on the other hand, work regularly, have a strong union, and win a larger share.

The level-of-coalition theory also explains wage differentials from one industry to another or from one area to another. Wages in the North are higher than in the South because industry is more highly unionized there. The very same jobs, in different plants of the same company, will show significant wage differentials between North and South.

But if the level of coalition is the main factor affecting levels of wages, what affects the level of coalition? Here there is a diversity of factors. Perhaps one of the most important is the extent of divisive factors like racism and sexism in the work force. For example, studies of prevailing wage levels in the United States suggest that where there is a higher degree of racism, wages of *white* workers tend to be lower.[17] This is difficult to explain in traditional theories but fits very naturally into the level-of-coalition theory.

A Note on Political Individualism

I have been arguing that the attempt to explain the distribution of income (and hence to justify it) in purely economic terms cannot succeed. On the other hand the theory I am proposing, the structural, level-of-coalition theory, although it does explain aspects of the distribution of income, does not lend itself to a justificatory theory at all. This is because the explaining factor ("having a high level of coalition") is ethically neutral. Farmworkers, doctors, and multinational oil companies have all increased their incomes by increasing their level of coalition. Consequently one cannot be said to be justified in having the results of all such coalitions.

Of course there are many other justificatory principles of distribution. If we think of them, with Nozick, as ways to fill in the blank in "to each according to ___ ," then a number of candidates suggest themselves: merit, need, and desert, for example, as well as the one I have been criticizing: contribution.[18]

But there is a certain criticism that could be made of them all: Who are *we*, after all, to be discussing how the social output should be divided up? Are we in charge of the distribution? There is a certain managerial point of view contained in all of them, for they all ask how the output should be distributed to individuals, and the question remains: Who is making this decision?

All discussion of the form Should we distribute according to X or according to Y? suffers from this managerial point of view. Rather, it could

---

17. See Michael Reich, "The Economics of Racism," in Michael Reich, Edwards, and Weisskopf, *The Capitalist System* (Englewood Cliffs, N.J.: Prentice-Hall, 1972.

18. See J. C. Dick, "How to Justify a Distribution of Earnings," *Philosophy and Public Affairs* 4, no. 3 (1975): 248.

be said, we should be asking how should society be structured so that people can decide how they want the distribution to be? In other words the discussion of economic distribution leaves out *politics.* The question of the structure of the process by which people decide what policies to implement is ignored in favor of the question What are the good policies?

This question raises the discussion to a higher level, the political level. It suggests that the justice of an economic policy does not lie in the shape of the distribution or in the attributes to which it is pegged but rather in the process by which the policy was generated: how it was arrived at, not what its content is. This gives us the foundation for a political theory of economic distribution. Here the concept of democracy is vital, a concept which is absent from most discussions of entitlements, especially those of the market theorists.

We are therefore led to pose the problem in the following way. What would be a method for *choosing* principles of distribution so that a policy chosen in that way would have some ethical justification? In viewing the problem in this way, we imagine a group of people making these choices based on their desires and preferences. Hence the problem becomes one of aggregation. Given a collection of individuals with various preferences, how can they determine a collective policy in a way that would lend justification to the outcome? Roughly speaking, this is the problem of political theory. An analysis of the various theories of democracy is beyond the scope of this book. I want merely to indicate a certain difficulty that I think infects a number of the discussions of the problem.

The difficulty is that the democratic problematic is framed as a situation in which we have a set of individuals $A_1, \ldots, A_n$ with "preference schedules" $P_1, \ldots, P_n$. We then look for a process by which they can choose an overall strategy. What is essential to this formulation is that we can at least imagine or make sense of the idea of an individual's preferences taken alone.

There is some reason to think that this cannot be done. People's preferences depend on *other* people's preferences, and so on. The presence of structural relations means that an individual's choices are not independent of the choices of others. The overall structure defines the possible moves or positions and their relations to one another. You can say that you prefer being rich to being poor, or vice versa, but the fact that *that* is the choice to be made and the fact that if some are rich then others cannot be, are structural conditions within which the choosing is done.

We might attempt to make even these facts be the subject of choice and might imagine a hypothetical collection of individuals choosing the principles that will govern the basic structure of society. This is the approach of Rawls's *A Theory of Justice.*

I want to examine Rawls's procedure for assessing the justice of principles. The basic construction is the notion of an *original position:* an idealized, hypothetical contracting situation made up of individuals who choose the principles of justice that are to govern their association in society.

The question then arises, On what basis do these contracting individuals choose one principle instead of another? Their own ethical intuitions? This would trivialize the situation immediately, for in the original position the utilitarians would choose utilitarianism, the libertarians would opt for the market, and so on. Clearly, if the theory is not going to be trivially circular, some way must be found to prevent the parties in the original position from simply voting their own pet ethical theories. This is accomplished in Rawls's system by the *veil of ignorance:* the parties are presumed not to know what their own conceptions of the good are.

A second element that must be blocked from the parties in the original position is any knowledge of their own particular interests, talents, abilities, or inclinations. If this were not done, the parties would be tempted to engage in special pleadings for their own interests disguised as universal principles. For example, the golfers would argue for lots of golf courses. So this sort of information, the kinds of things which separate one person's interests from another's, are assumed to be blocked from the individuals by the veil of ignorance.

We might ask, What is left? If the parties do not know their own interests and do not know their own conceptions of the good, what would make them choose one thing over anything else? Rawls's answer is contained in the notion of *primary goods,* which are "things that every rational man is presumed to want." He says, "Regardless of what an individual's rational plans are in detail, it is assumed that there are various things which he would prefer more of rather than less" (p. 92).

This takes care of the second problem, that of differing individual conceptions of interests; all persons are assumed to be interested in the primary goods. Examples of these are: "rights and liberties, powers and opportunities, income and wealth." (Rawls adds: "Later on the primary good of self-respect has a central place.") But we have not yet taken care of the first problem, namely, on the basis of what kind of principle of choice the individuals will do their choosing.

Here Rawls makes a certain crucial assumption. In order to avoid the circularity of having the original position contaminated by the private ethical theories of the participants, Rawls assumes that they are purely self-interested. They choose a principle of justice on the basis of the amount of primary good it will deliver *to them.* Each party is attempting to maximize its own share in the distribution. He says: "They are conceived as not taking an interest in one another's interests." Each party, then, chooses a principle that will maximize its own payoff, except of course it does not know *who* it will be.

Rawls suggests that in such a situation the strategic thing to do is to choose defensively. If you do not know who you are going to be, it is wise to order society so that the worst possible situation is as good as it can be. That way you will cover the worst-case possibility that *you* will become that person. An example of this kind of reasoning is provided by the way we learned as children to divide up a cake: one person cuts, and the other person chooses. The cutter defends against the worst-case outcome (likely in this case) by cutting two equal pieces. By a similar logic Rawls concludes that the parties to the original position would choose equality as their principle for the distribution of liberties. Indeed, one might be tempted to say that one would always choose an equal distribution of everything, but this would not be true, according to Rawls.

For suppose that there was a certain kind of *in*equality in which every single person was better off than in any equal distribution. In other words, suppose that for some reason one had to choose between two different distributions over three people. In the first distribution the payoff schedule is

$$A = 3$$
$$B = 3 \qquad \text{(I)}$$
$$C = 3$$

and in the second distribution it is

$$A = 4$$
$$B = 5 \qquad \text{(II)}$$
$$C = 10.$$

Leave aside the problem of how it is that there are exactly these choices or how it is that the total product in the two cases is different. Just ask which of the two you would prefer. Clearly, you would take II because no matter how the lottery turned out you would be better off with the worst alternative under II than with any chance under I.[19]

Rawls's suggestion, then, is that with respect to the economic distribution, the principle of justice which the parties would choose would not be total equality but rather would tolerate inequality when that inequality would yield a greater payoff to everyone, in particular, to the worst-off person (the worst-case possibility). So it turns out that the principles of justice so chosen allow for inequalities under these conditions. (Rawls calls this the difference principle.)

But is not the basic form of argument right? Would you not rather be in a 4–5–10 lottery than a 3–3–3 one? As Rawls realizes, the crucial assumption here is that each individual is interested only in increasing his own payoff, that is, that we "take no interest in the interests of others." After all, it would be possible to imagine someone saying: "If we had the second system, then if I were the one who was A, it would bother me that other people had much more than I did. Even though I would have more than in the first system, it would spoil it for me that others had so much more still."

Rawls wants to exclude such an attitude from the original position. The principle that we take no interest in the interests of others has as a corollary the nonexistence of *envy* in the original position.

But if the numbers in the payoff schedules represent general levels of holdings, there is more than just envy as a reason to fear the inegalitarian distribution. This may seem odd, for what except envy could make you care that someone has more than you? Well, one very important class of

---

19. Although this choice situation is being discussed in the abstract, it may help to see what an application of it might be. It has been suggested that the difference between socialism and capitalism is essentially the difference between I and II. Under socialism there is economic equality, the argument runs, but that results in a low level of incentive to produce and therefore a smaller social product. Under capitalism, on the other hand, there is inequality but the great incentive to get a larger share results in a larger social pie to be divided. Thus everyone benefits, some of course more than others. So the argument goes. There are quite a number of very substantial theoretical assumptions being made here, about the nature of incentives, about the distribution of income under capitalism, and so on. All of them are debatable, to say the least.

cases in which you would care is if the level of holding of the other person enabled that person to affect *your* well-being.

Rawls is obviously not thinking about this kind of good. He is thinking about consumer goods, and for goods that one takes home and consumes, the principle Who cares how much others have? makes sense. If I would get only half a sandwich for lunch in the first system, and a whole sandwich in the second, what do I care if someone else gets five sandwiches? This works fine with sandwiches. But suppose that the quantities in question are, for example, *levels of armaments*. Now the situation is quite different. The person in the original position ought to reason as follows. In system I all of us will have three guns. Therefore there will be a balance of terror, and no one will be able to dominate anyone else. But in system II person C will dominate the others, hence system II will be a dictatorship. So system I is preferable.

In other words there are many kinds of goods for which the independence assumptions of the original position are not satisfied where it is rational to be concerned with how much other people have because there are *internal relations* between the level of one's holdings and the levels of others' holdings.

Level of armaments is only an example. And of course, strictly speaking, the quantity of armaments I have does not change if someone else gets more. Rather, what changes is the degree of security which I have. I still have three guns, only it does not achieve the level of security that it did before.

The crucial point is that there are many important kinds of quantities which do not obey the independence assumption. Certainly, notions like political and legal *power* do not. One's political power is one's ability to press claims in the political arena, that is, to press claims against other people. Similarly, the degree of one's ability to buy legal representation measures one's ability to press claims in the law against other people. Therefore, the more political representation you have, the less I have. This is not because senators are a scarce resource or because power is like haute couture, appealing only because so few can afford it, but because the basic nature of political power is that it is the ability to affect others.

Consequently, with respect to any situation which exhibits these sorts of internal relations, the argument for a benign inequality collapses. But there are many situations like this, especially the distribution of political power. The situation can even arise with respect to the economic distribution itself because if one person's share is much larger than another's, that person will have various kinds of market power over the second.

This means that the distribution of political power cannot be subject to the difference principle. But the problem is that political power, as such, does not come up for discussion at all. There is talk about political liberties and about economic shares but not about the way in which one's economic share affects one's ability to exercise political liberties.

This is not so much an objection to Rawls as it is a warning against certain applications. The theory simply does not apply to these kinds of situations, and this, in turn, means that the question of economic inequality will have to be taken up with a more sophisticated appreciation of its consequences. In particular the whole question of the relationship between political equality and economic inequality will have to be rethought. Rawls, characteristic of the liberal tradition, separates the two, but this obviously creates problems in situations where they interact.[20]

20. A good discussion of some of these problems can be found in Norman Daniels's essay "Equal Liberty and Unequal Worth of Liberty," in Norman Daniels, ed., *Reading Rawls* (New York: Basic Books, 1975).

4 Biology and Society

The Model of Individual Differences: Social Darwinism

The market model addressed the question Why is there inequality? and interpreted it as a question about explaining levels of holdings. The focus was on the activities which produced the holdings rather than on the individuals themselves. The question was, Why does a given individual have this level of holdings rather than some other level? The thing to be explained was a concrete distribution, and the explanatory focus was placed on the sequence of events (trades) that led to that distribution. The more political approach represented by Rawls asked for the justification not of particular distributions but of principles of distribution. But the focus was still on the process as the explanation of inequality rather than on the characteristics of the individuals taking part in it.

The kind of explanation that I want to talk about in this chapter is a kind of figure/ground reversal of the previous schemes, for it places the explanatory focus on characteristics of the individuals instead of on the process. It looks for stable properties of individuals as answers to the question

What is it in virtue of which one individual rather than another comes to occupy a social position?

The kind of answers I will study are answers which explain these distributions by citing differences in these individual characteristics. This class of explanations is a large and important family and ranges over a wide variety. Consider explanations which seek to answer the question

Why are some people poor?

and think of the variety of answers that have been given. Some answers lay the blame on the poor themselves and attribute poverty to character flaws. The social Darwinist William Graham Sumner said that the poor

lack the necessary "industry, prudence, continence or temperance."
Sir Francis Galton, a pioneer of IQ testing, wrote: "The men who
achieve eminence and those who are naturally capable are, to a large
extent, identical."[1] The variety runs from moralistic answers like these
to explanations of the liberal kind, citing factors such as "low educational level" or "cultural deprivation," or conservative ones in terms
of hereditary IQ or other innate cognitive traits.

For my purposes here, what they all have in common is that they
try to explain an individual fact,

Why A has P,

by appeal to another fact,

because A has Q.

I think that there is something wrong with all these explanations, a
defect which derives from their very form. I will use as a paradigm of
such explanations a somewhat stylized version of Plato's *Republic*.
The ideal society that Socrates describes consists of three classes (call
them X, Y, and Z) with definite structural relations among them and
definite numerical proportions. Let us represent this structure graphically
as

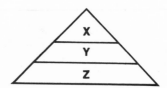

Now suppose we were to ask what explains why an individual ends up
in one class rather than another. At one point this is taken up as an
ideological problem, a problem in public relations: What shall we tell
the people when they ask? The answer, Socrates says, is to tell them a
"noble lie":

> All of you in the city are certainly brothers, we shall say to them in
> telling the tale, but the god, in fashioning those of you who are com-
> petent to rule, mixed gold in at their birth; this is why they are most

1. Cited by R. Hofstadter, *Social Darwinism in American Thought* (New York:
George Braziller, 1955), p. 164.

honored; in auxiliaries, silver; and iron and bronze in the farmers and other craftsmen. (415a, Bloom trans.)

That is, the class structure of the society is to be seen as the straightforward causal product of another underlying structure, namely, the underlying distribution of metals in the soul at birth. The explanation of the social fortunes of individuals in the city then takes a coherent form. The answer to the question

Why is A in class X (Y, Z)?

is

because A's soul contains G (S, B).

My concern here is not with the details of Plato's argument or the specific characteristics of the classes which comprise the city but with the fact that an individual's social class is explained by appeal to some other property of the individual, and that this explaining property is inherent in the individual.

Now, of course, "gold," "silver," and "bronze" are not to be taken literally; this is a myth. But what is Plato's actual explanation for why an individual occupies a given social role? It turns out that the actual explanation is not very different from the myth. The early part of book II is devoted to the construction of the ideal city. There Socrates makes a number of statements to the effect that an individual's social position is the result of natural or innate capacities. At the beginning of the argument he says, "Each of us is naturally not quite like anyone else, but rather differs in his nature; different men are apt for the accomplishment of different jobs" (370a). And at the conclusion of his construction of the city he says again: "To each one of the others we assigned one thing, the one for which his nature fitted him, at which he was to work throughout his life" (374c). In other words the noble lie occurs twice in the *Republic*: in the middle of the book in its mythological form but also early in the book, demythologized, as an asserted premise necessary for Plato's argument.

This naturalistic explanation of social inequality can stand proxy for more contemporary accounts, which have the same basic form. They differ mostly in the kinds of stratification they seek to explain, and in the details of the mechanisms by which the inherent properties are supposed to surface as the causes of social positions.

One of the main examples of this form of explanation is that of social

Darwinism, in which the individual properties that explain social status are Sumner's "industry, prudence, continence or temperance." Other examples include the later eugenicists, for whom poverty was explained by "feeble mindedness" and the contemporary (neo-)social Darwinists, for whom IQ is the explanation of social status. In each of these cases, as in Plato's *Republic*, a set of social facts about the overall distribution of positions in society is explained by appeal to an antecedent individualistic property or distribution of properties.

The critique of these explanations is based on this fact. In order to make this critique, let me review some of the conclusions about explanation from the end of chapter 1. First, every explanation has presuppositions which serve to limit the alternatives to the phenomenon being explained. Second, in some cases the presuppositions take a special form. Recall the discussion of the class being graded on a curve. There was exactly one A to be given out to the class, and it turned out that Mary was the one who got it. Now it is possible to ask

Why did Mary get an A?

and get an answer like

She wrote a good final.

Yet this answer is misleading, I argued, for if we asked, counterfactually, what would have been the case if everyone had written a good final, the answer is *not* that everyone would have gotten an A. The fact that if everyone had written a good final, not everyone would have gotten an A, means that there are structural presuppositions at work in framing the question. The "real" question being answered is not

Why did Mary get an A?

but rather the question

Why, given that someone was to get an A, was it *Mary*?

In general I argued that in every case where the generalized counterfactual is false, the space of social possibilities is not "free" but has strong presupposed constraints.

Turning to the social Darwinist explanations of social position, we find a similar phenomenon. Suppose the question is why the rich are rich and the answer is "prudence, industry and thrift." We must then ask, well, what if everyone were prudent, industrious, and thrifty? Would everyone be rich? The answer is obviously no. Consequently, "prudence, industry, and thrift" cannot possibly be an answer to the question

Why are some people rich?

simpliciter, but, *at best,* an answer to the restricted question:

Why, given that some are rich, it is *these* people and not others?

The same general point applies to explanations of social position which are not strictly social Darwinist in character, because they appeal to *environmental* individual facts rather than innate ones. Consider, for example, explanations of unemployment, such as "low educational level," which appeal to environmental characteristics of the unemployed. These also have the form of explaining

Why A is U

by appealing to a fact that has the form

Because A is L.

Applying again the test for structural presuppositions, we consider the two counterfactuals:

If everyone had a low educational level, everyone would be unemployed.

and

If no one had a low educational level, no one would be unemployed.

Both of these are false, and so we can conclude that the space of social possibilities is not free but has presupposed constraints, and that what is really getting explained is

Why, given that someone is to be unemployed, is it *Harold*?

We have, therefore, two different questions here, and the individual characteristics answer is at best an answer to the second question. The presuppositions, of internal relations among the individual destinies, make the two questions diverge:

1. Why is there this distribution?

and

2. Why, given this distribution, does one individual occupy a given place in it rather than another?

If there were no structural presuppositions, the overall possibility-space would be independent, and the two questions would coincide. Consider, for example, the property of being red-haired. Suppose 15 percent of the population has red hair. Then the explanation of why 15 percent of the population has red hair is individualistic. We explain of each of them, individualistically, why he or she has red hair, and the overall explanation is just the logical sum of the individualistic ones.

The crucial fact is the independence of the things to be explained. Red hair is purely independent: one person's having red hair does not decrease the likelihood of another's having red hair. But this is typically not the case for the kinds of predicates that are the objects of social explanation. For example, in the case of unemployment, economic theory tells us that some employment is ineliminable, and that there are structural relations between unemployment levels and other economic variables in virtue of which the unemployment of one person is not purely independent of the unemployment of another. There is, for example, the law known as the Phillips curve, which asserts a fixed trade-off between the unemployment rate and the inflation rate: Unemployment can be decreased only at the expense of an increase in the inflation rate, which in turn rebounds on other economic variables, including the unemployment rate itself.

This nonindependence, signaled by the failure of the generalized counterfactual (What if everyone had property P?), means that the two questions diverge. Let us call them, respectively, the structural question and the individualistic question.

How is the structural question answered? It is instructive to look at the *Republic* in this regard. Is it true that if all people had gold in their souls, everyone would be in class I? No. The three-class structure of the city has an independent explanation and therefore a reason for being which transcends the makeup of the individuals who comprise it. Recall the beginning of book II, where Socrates and the others are launching into the construction of the ideal society. Their method is to build up an economically self-sufficient society, and their arguments are from what might be called the theory of economic organization. They concern what overall social needs have to be filled and how best to fill them. Socrates says things like, "Well, the first and greatest of needs is the provision of food for existing and living. . . . Won't one man be a farmer, another the housebuilder, still another the weaver?" (369d). Later on, similar kinds of considerations are advanced to explain why a class of guardians is needed, why a class of auxiliaries, the size of those classes, and their respective interrelations. The latter is especially important, for it is in the structural interrelations of the classes that justice lies.

In other words, relying on the distinction between structural and individualistic questions, we can say that we have here a nontrivial answer to the structural question Why this structure? The answer is: The various classes, proportions, and interrelations are necessary to the harmonious functioning of society. The explanation is purely in terms of considerations of a social nature.

But this leaves us with an enormous problem. The distribution of individual social abilities is explained by the innate gold, silver, and bronze. (Or, less mythologically, the distribution of farmers, auxiliaries, and so forth is explained by their innate "natures.") Then we have a completely different account, the explanation of the structure of society, in terms of social "needs." This gives us another, independent derivation of the necessary structure of society. What is remarkable, and inexplicable, is that *these two structures coincide perfectly.* The social structure, derived from the theory of economic organization, corresponds exactly to the available distribution of innate types. It turns out that there are exactly as many openings for class I people as there are potential candidates, and similarly for the other classes.

Why should this be the case? There is no reason. It is something of a miracle: the perfect correspondence of biology with the needs of this or that form of social organization. We could call it the Immaculate Conception of Social Roles. It is a miracle which, it turns out, occurs crucially at just about the same place in every social Darwinist account.

The problem is that there is always some presupposition of social structure in any attempt to explain social positions. Social Darwinism fails to see this and attempts to explain social position purely in biological terms. This is impossible. Social Darwinism tells us that the structure of society is explained by the antecedent distribution of innate types. The presuppositions of such an explanation are that the social environment in which these inherent traits are expressed is *neutral* with respect to their actualization. For example, suppose the question is why there is a certain distribution of height in society, and the explanation cites an antecedent distribution of "height genes." Then the presupposition is that the environment is neutral with respect to the actualization of these innate tendencies. It could not be the case, for example, that the environment encouraged the development of height potential in some but retarded it in others, for if it were, we could not explain the distribution of height in this way.

The presupposition of neutrality entails that the actualization of one person's inner essence is independent of the actualization of another person's inner essence. But in the cases where the structure is already given by external considerations, like the teacher's decision in the case of grading on a curve, or social "needs" in the *Republic*, this independence cannot be satisfied. When a structure is imposed from without, the resulting nonindependence of the individuals means that we cannot have an individualistic cause of a nonindividualistic effect. One of two things must be the case:
either

1. the causes really are individualistic, in which case we have the problem of the correspondence miracle,

or

2. the properties cited as causes are not really independent and hence cannot be biological.[2]

The latter situation occurs in the grading example, where the explanation of

why Mary got an A

was, really, a disguised relative term, denoting a property of Mary *relative to* the other people in the class (e.g., "wrote a better final than anyone else").

Social Darwinism as an explanation is caught between these two alternatives. On the one hand, many social Darwinists suggest that they have no fixed preconceptions or presuppositions about the structure of society or the distribution of social goods; they assume or state explicitly that if everyone had the desirable qualities, everyone would be happy. Certainly, this is a necessary assumption for eugenicists who propose to eliminate poverty and other ills by eliminating supposed

2. I am assuming here that biological factors are necessarily individualistic. This is certainly true of the examples we are considering. There is, however, a strong case to be made for a nonindividualistic biology, whose basic units would be groups, species, or even ecosystems. See V. C. Wynne-Edwards, "Intergroup Selection in the Evolution of Social Systems" Nature 200 (1963): 623–26.

genetic causes. For all social Darwinists, eugenicists or not, the basic assumption is that there is no socially imposed pattern on the distribution of individual fortunes; society allows people to fulfill their (biological) destinies except, of course, where that is interfered with by the meddling of do-gooders. This kind of liberty or independence of individual fortunes is one of the crucial assumptions of social Darwinism. Sumner writes:

> If, then, there be liberty, men get from her [nature] just in proportion to their works, and their having and enjoying are just in proportion to their being and doing. . . . We can deflect the penalties of those who have done ill and throw them on those who have done better. . . . [But] the latter carries society downward and favors all its worst members. (p. 76)

Now what is curious is that the other major assumption of social Darwinism, that society is competitive, flatly contradicts this independence assumption. I want to make out this claim in some detail. All social Darwinists, classical and contemporary, make the competitiveness of society a crucial premise in their argument; Sumner, for example, writes: "Competition, therefore, is a law of nature. Nature is entirely neutral; she submits to him who most energetically and resolutely assails her." (p. 76) This is the essence of what they take to be Darwinism: that nature is a competitive struggle and therefore that the fittest survive.

But there is a serious confusion at work here. Let us say that a practice is *weakly* competitive if each participant struggles against nature, receives an outcome, and the outcomes are then compared. Golf is weakly competitive: each of us goes out and gets our own scores, and the results are then compared for competitions. On the other hand, a *strongly* competitive situation is one in which I achieve my score in struggle with you and only by depriving you of it. Tennis is strongly competitive. The critical fact about these two kinds of situations is that in weakly competitive situations individualistic explanations suffice, whereas they are inadequate to explain strongly competitive situations. If A defeats B in golf and the question arises Why did A win and B lose?, the answer is simply the logical sum of the two independent explanations of the score which A received and the score which B received. But if A defeats B in tennis there is no such thing as the independent explanations of why A defeated B on the one hand and why B lost to A on the other. There is only one, unified explanation of the outcome of the match.

Social Darwinists make a great deal out of the competitiveness of society and go so far as to say that this fact accounts for the survival of the fittest, but they are confusing the two notions of competition. Sumner speaks above about the struggle against nature as a struggle which is, in our terms, weakly competitive. He wishes to use the form of explanation which is appropriate to those situations, for he immediately says that the individual's density is the result only of properties of that individual. But if anything is clear it is that society is not weakly, but strongly, competitive and the presence of strong competition ensures that there are internal relations among the individual destinies of the participants. Consequently, individualistic explanation will not suffice in such cases.

What is surprising is that Sumner even notices this distinction between the two kinds of competition but fails to see its significance:

> There is first the struggle of individuals to win the means of subsistence
> from nature, and secondly there is the competition of man with man in
> the effort to win a limited supply. The radical error of the socialists
> and sentimentalists is that they never distinguish these two relations from
> each other. They bring forward complaints which are really to be
> made, if at all, against the author of the universe for the hardships
> which man has to endure in his struggle with nature. (p. 16)

He seems to take it as obvious that social inequality is due to weak competition (the differential skills with which we all pursue some independent tasks) and not strong competition (necessary or structural inequality). Yet it is evident that at least some of the basic inequalities of society are the product of the strong competition inherent in the structure. This is the thrust of Rousseau's *Discourse on the Origin of Inequality,* which was discussed in the previous chapter. Rousseau's claim is that conflicting interests in society, the fact that one generally gains at the expense of another, means that certain forms of individualistic explanation cannot work. In the previous chapter it meant that the Lockean program of justifying entitlements individual by individual will not work. Here it means that the social Darwinist program of explaining (and justifying) success individual by individual also will not work. Such conflicts are essential to capitalist society, where, Rousseau says, "We find our advantage in the detriment of our fellow-men, and someone's loss almost always creates another's prosperity. . . . Some want illness, others death, others war, others famine."[3]

The important question seems to be Why are there these interrelations? A great deal of social inequality follows from them alone, yet this question is not faced by social Darwinists.

A similar problem haunts contemporary social Darwinism as well. There is a great deal of talk about individual differences but very little about where social structure comes from.

Perhaps the best example of this is Herrnstein's "IQ," which, when it appeared in 1971, became one of the focal points of the contemporary revival of social Darwinism. His claim is that IQ, which he equates with "intelligence," is the factor which explains an individual's success in society. High IQ people, he says, tend to occupy positions with high "earnings and prestige." But just as in the *Republic,* we need an explanation over and above this one, an explanation of why a particular social structure is the case. And, just as in Plato, we find a second theory working quietly alongside the theory of individual differences. This second theory is a sociopolitical theory about what kinds of social structures we should have. In Herrnstein's case it consists of a set of assertions, on the last page of the article, about why we need hierarchically organized societies with large differential rewards. We need them, he says, because "ability expresses itself in labor only for gain" and because "human society has yet to find a working alternative to the carrot and the stick."

It is this theory which is really doing the work of explaining why society is and should be stratified. But what *is* this theory? As it exists here, it is a collection of homilies, which geneticist Richard Lewontin ridicules as "barroom widsom." We could try to work it up into a theory, although notions like "gain" and "the carrot and the stick" have proved notoriously difficult and controversial. Perhaps one way to put the claim would be this: the best, most efficient, allocation of resources is achieved by ordering social positions hierarchically, establishing a system of differential rewards reflecting that hierarchy, and thereby recruiting the most highly skilled to the jobs we want them to pursue at the upper end of the hierarchy.

As a piece of social theorizing there are a remarkable number of

3. J. J. Rousseau, *Discourse on the Origin of Inequality,* ed. R. D. Masters (New York: St. Martin's Press, 1964), p. 194.

presuppositions contained in this picture. Some large theoretical assumptions are swallowed whole: theories about what kinds of incentives work in what kinds of situations, theories about what sorts of things motivate people, theories about job skills and the causes of job performance, as well as theories of organization and collective behavior. All these theories are debatable, to say the least. The size and difficulty of the questions they involve indicate the magnitude of the assumptions which the hierarchical theory makes. A proper discussion of the question Why this structure? would have to begin by raising these kinds of questions.[4]

Genetics and Social Causality
The basic claim I am making is that social structure is radically underdetermined by individual differences. Since biological differences are the paradigm case of individual differences, it follows that biological differences, by themselves, can never fully explain social structure. The explanatory frame

> biology ⟶ society

always contains a suppressed presupposition of social structure, so it is elliptical for a more correct explanation:

> biology X society ⟶ society.

I want to study in detail how this affects claims of genetic causality. First of all, to begin with the obvious, any genetic cause whatever must have a certain environment in order to produce its effect. Without a womb environment of the right kind, no genetic trait can cause anything. This much is elementary.

But there are other ways in which the causality is dependent on the social environment, ways that are less obvious. Here is a simple illustration from standard genetic theory. There is a disease called phenylketonuria (PKU), which is an inability to metabolize the protein phenylalanine. This in turn causes overt symptoms. The disease PKU is caused by a genetic defect. That is, the presence of a certain gene causes an inability to metabolize phenylalanine (in the standard womb

4. See Noam Chomsky, "Psychology and Ideology," *Cognition* 1 (1972): 11, for a discussion of the dubious sociological assumptions contained in Herrnstein's argument.

environments; if genetic surgery were possible, even this causal link could be broken). But the inability to metabolize phenylalanine causes the gross symptoms of PKU only in a certain range of postnatal environments, namely, those consisting of normal diets, which contain phenylalanine. If the baby is placed on a diet free of phenylalanine, no gross symptoms occur, and the baby is fine. It still cannot metabolize phenylalanine but then it does not have to.

So it would be a mistake to say

genetics $\longrightarrow$ PKU.

The more correct explanatory frame would include the double dependence on two different environments thus:

genetics $\times$ womb environment $\longrightarrow$ trait T

and

trait T $\times$ normal diet $\longrightarrow$ PKU,

where T stands for "inability to metabolize phenylalanine."

So far, all this is familiar. But there is yet another way in which such claims of genetic causality have structural presuppositions, and the examination of it will cast some doubt on the kinds of inferences which have been made by the proponents of biological explanations in social theory.

Consider a society which is like our own except that a confiscatory income tax is passed which applies only to redheaded people. If we assume that red hair is a genetic trait, we get the surprising conclusion that, in that society, poverty is "caused" by a genetic trait. Now, of course, this is true only in a somewhat backhanded sense. Being redhaired, we want to say, does not really *cause* poverty; that would be misleading to say. Instead, we would say, being red-haired causes one to be discriminated against by that society. The *real* cause of poverty is the social discrimination.[5]

Consequently, we must add to the double dependence on social structure a third presupposition, the presupposed background of social practices. The first two presuppositions can be put as

---

5. For a discussion of a similar point, see N. J. Block and G. Dworkin, "IQ, Heritability and Inequality II," in N. J. Block and G. Dworkin, eds., *The IQ Argument* (New York: Pantheon Books, 1976), p. 49.

genetics × womb environment ⟶ trait T

trait T × developmental environment ⟶ individual property I,

and this third dimension can be put as

individual property I × social environment (rules of the game) ⟶
social position S.

The trouble with the standard claims of genetic causality in social
theory is that they suppress these presuppositions and thus paint a
false picture of the causalities involved. This suppression is made possible
by a certain very general view of the nature of causality itself. All the
pioneers of IQ research have been hard-line empiricists with regard to
causality. Just as Hume banished causality as metaphysical and analyzed
its scientific content into spatiotemporal contiguity and especially
constant conjunction, so modern empiricists have banished the term
causality and replaced it with the current analogue of Hume's constant
conjunction, namely, correlation. We are told that the correlation
between two variables is all we can scientifically expect.

This is a curious view. Partly it is based on an erroneous view of the
role of causality in the physical sciences; many empiricists believe,
falsely, that physical science has eliminated the concept of causality.
In fact that is not true: physical science may not use the word *causality*,
but causal concepts are certainly there and are operating in statements like "Mu mesons bind the proton to the nucleus." And of
course there are plenty of causal terms sprinkled throughout the IQ
discussion; the net effect of the skepticism about causality has been
not to dispense with causal assumptions but to dispense with talking about them.[6]

We cannot really dispense with causality because, among other things,
it is the basis for making any practical recommendations whatever.
Any strategy for intervention in the world, any strategy for changing
anything, must of necessity be based on causal information, not just
correlations. The light's being on in a room is highly correlated with
the light switch's being in the ON position, but if you are interested in
making the light go on or off, you need more information than that
correlation. You need the asymmetric fact that one of those things is
the cause of the other not the symmetric fact that they are correlated.

6. Again, see Block and Dworkin, pts. I and II, for a good discussion of this
point.

Certainly, the proponents of IQ must, despite what they say, believe in at least *some* causal relations. Jensen, for example, believes that the reason why "compensatory education has . . . failed" is that low IQ in black children is *caused* by genetic factors. If drawing causal conclusions were really forbidden, none of these writers could make any of the claims about the causes of stratification that they obviously want to make. Their skepticism has the effect of allowing them to have their cake and eat it too. They can make all sorts of claims about what sorts of intervention strategies will and will not work, based on substantial causal assumptions, and then, when those assumptions are challenged, can reply, "Well, what is causality anyway, but a metaphysical notion?"

It is instructive in this regard to look at the notion of genetic causality which is used in these discussions. When it is claimed that IQ is caused by genetic differences, the notion that is being used is a statistical notion, *heritability*.

The claim which is made for popular consumption as "genetics causes social position" is more accurately stated as "differences in social position are heritable." This notion of heritability is crucial to the claims of the contemporary social Darwinists. I will not attempt here a full discussion of this notion. It is certainly a fascinating case study in the philosophy of science and is perhaps the best example of the failure of statistical, correlational concepts to capture causal notions.[7] My purpose here is to focus on a single aspect of that issue.

The heritability of a trait in a population is defined as the amount of variation in that trait which is due to genetic variation. The trouble with the definition is that is uses the concept "due to," a causal concept. This causality is analyzed away statistically by talking instead about correlations between genetic variation, on the one hand, and variation in the trait, on the other.

But this slide into correlationism is fatal because it suppresses just the things we need to know: the true causalities which underlie these correlations. In the case of the society which discriminates against redheaded people, poverty has a high heritability because it is highly correlated with a genetic trait, red hair. But this is misleading. Intuitively, there are two distinct types of situation: on the one hand,

---

7. See R. Lewontin, "The Analysis of Variance and the Analysis of Causes," in Block and Dworkin, eds., *The IQ Argument,* for a discussion of the relation between heritability and causality.

the situation where there really is some genetic cause of poverty, and on the other, the type above, where the cause of poverty is social discrimination. *By its nature the concept of heritability cannot distinguish between the two.* Since it is a correlational notion, it cannot distinguish between two different causal configurations underlying the same covariance of the genetic trait and the social property.

We can begin to recognize a certain fallacy at work in the social Darwinist argument. A property is considered which is really a structural property (e.g., being poor). Then the structural condition is quietly presupposed, and one begins to ask how individual differences contribute to differences with respect to that property. The structural condition is thereby "built into" the individuals.

In addition to its other defects, an explanatory frame like this gives a false picture of the causalities involved and hence a false picture of the ways in which we could intervene to change the situation.

How to Explain Social Stratification Structurally

I argued in the previous pages that there cannot be an individualistic answer to the question Why is there a given social structure? and, therefore, that social stratification cannot be explained by appeal to an antecedent "natural" stratification. The question then arises of how one *does* explain social structure, in particular, how we are to explain social stratification?

The social Darwinist kind of explanation of stratification proceeds by postulating differences among the individuals who are assigned to different strata. The kind of explanation I am going to suggest is unusual in that it makes no such assumption; I will sketch an explanation of social stratification which assumes an underlying homogeneity, an explanation which assumes no significant individual differences. Later I will discuss the importance of this. First is the explanation itself.

Consider the protocapitalist market, the ur-market of the early classical economists like Adam Smith. As we discussed in chapter 3, its essential features are that it is a collection of small entrepreneurs in a competitive market, a homogeneous collection of traders engaged in competition with one another for resources or markets. The crucial fact about this situation is that it is *unstable.* In fact, as the degree of competition sharpens, the homogeneous situation becomes less and less stable. Many factors contribute to this situation:

1. The fact that the system is competitive means that small differences will be reinforced in a positive feedback. If A and B are competing entrepreneurs, a small advantage which A might gain over B enables him to gain a greater competitive edge over B, and thereby to increase the gap between them. For example, if A has a larger stake than B, he can set his prices below cost, temporarily, in order to drive B out of business. This strategy, predatory pricing, was one of the main strategies John D. Rockefeller used to build up Standard Oil. Or he can use this larger stake to buy up more modern machinery or to corner or partially corner markets or raw materials.

2. The existence of *economies of scale* also contributes to the instability. Large-scale production is simply more efficient than small-scale; more automation can be used, supplies can be bought in larger quantities, and so on. Hence a small advantage tends to become bigger.

3. There are other advantages to the larger firm which help make it still larger and to drive out the smaller firms. The larger firm can buy advertising, legal representation, and political influence that the smaller cannot.

4. There is also the sensitivity of the situation to what are called *coalitional strategies*. Anyone who has played Monopoly knows that as the game advances, it becomes more and more tempting to the players to form coalitions, in which A and B pool their resources to wipe out C and share the spoils. This is another important factor reducing the number of competitors and producing a concentration of holdings. (The rules of Monopoly prohibit such coalitions, but no serious player feels constrained by the petit bourgeois moralism of Parker Brothers.)

All these factors, working together, result in the instability of the society of homogeneous small entrepreneurs. It necessarily stratifies because each of the entrepreneurs is trying hard to use these methods and, more, to eliminate the competition. This is not a statement about their psychology as much as it is about the rules of the game. If A declines to attempt to eliminate the competition, this contributes directly to the likelihood of A's being eliminated. "Get them before they get you" is not a prior psychological malady of the traders; it is a theorem in the strategy theory of the game.

So the initial situation of equality is unstable and, like a supersaturated solution, it tends to crystallize into a more stable mode consisting of a large number of more or less impoverished people and a small residue into which the original capital has agglomerated. In the initial state everyone is a small entrepreneur, but the force of competition has made that state unstable. Most of the small traders get wiped out and become sellers of (their) labor. On the other hand, capital concentrates in the remaining few.[8] This gives the resulting system a different overall dynamics.

The form of this explanation is important. It says that, under given conditions, the market will develop into a new mode in which there are a few holders of capital and many sellers of labor, but it makes no attempt to say *who* they will be. It explains a stratification without assuming a prior difference in the underlying medium.

In a way this may seem impossible, a violation of causality or of the principle of sufficient reason. How can differences emerge from the undifferentiated? Does this not violate classical determinism? In a certain sense the answer is yes. Classical determinism tells us that there must be some differences in the underlying medium or the initial state.

Nevertheless, I think this principle should be rejected. The reasons are essentially those of chapter 2: even if there is supposed to be a complete underlying determinism, it is so *unstable* as to be useless. What we want to know are the stable relations, and for this we must renounce the possibility of explaining deterministically why the system differentiated at this point rather than that.

Such explanations are very powerful because they show that the stratification is really explained by the structure, not by the individuals. An explanation which gives us a purely structural answer to the question Why is there social stratification? tells us that such stratification is part of the inherent dynamics of the system, a consequence of the geometry of social relations. By explaining the existence of stratification in the absence of any individual differences, it tells us that stratification like this would occur even if there were no individual differences of any consequence. This pulls the rug out from under individualistic explanations for stratification because it shows that the stratification would have taken place in any case.

8. It is interesting to note how concentrated capital has become. In 1969 there were 300,000 U.S. corporations. The 500 largest (i.e., one-sixth of 1% of the total) had 60% of the total sales and 70% of the profits.

And yet the question will not go away. Must there not be *some* difference between the individuals who become members of the one stratum rather than the other?

Recall our distinction between the two different questions that can be asked about a social structure:

1. Why is there this structure? (structural question),

and

2. Why, given this structure, does an individual come to occupy a given place in it? (individualistic question).

We can agree that "individual differences" cannot answer the structural question, but must it not be the answer to the second question? The structural explanation, in addition to giving us an answer to the first question, also suggests the weakness of individual-differences explanations *even as answers to the second question.*

Consider a substance in supersaturated solution, cooled to a temperature T. We know that for values of T beyond some critical value T_0, part of the substance will be precipitated out as a residue. Suppose A_0 is one of those molecules. Then, analogously to the social case, we may ask

1. Why did the solution precipitate? (Answer: because T was less than T_0)

and

2. Why did it precipitate out A_0?

It looks as if the answer to the second question would have to be in terms of individual differences, something that distinguished A_0 from the other molecules.

The problem is that there may be no such property or, at least, it may be unknowable whether A_0 actually possesses such a property. After all, as T approaches the critical point, the necessary difference between a molecule and its neighbors, in virtue of which it will be selected as the precipitate, becomes less and less and eventually vanishes to zero. The system, we might say, becomes less and less choosy about *where* it is going to precipitate. Near the limit, anything will do. Microscopic differences, finally even quantum differences, will select out a molecule as part of the residue.

So, in a case like this, the structural answer may be all the answer there is, even to the individualistic question. The best answer that can be given to the question Why did it precipitate at A_0? may be "because it had to precipitate somewhere." It will not help to insist "but there *must* be some difference, else why *there*?" because this difference may be infinitesimal, of a kind which is unknown, and whose nature cannot be nontrivially stated.

The explanation of social stratification is similar. If we do have a good structural explanation of why a certain kind of stratification must occur, we can say that such stratification will be imposed on whatever individual properties there are. If there are not any significant differences, the system will find some, invent some, or elevate some insignificant differences to a decisive role. To the extent to which there is a structural explanation of inequality, the individual-differences explanation becomes less and less plausible.

So there may be good reasons for avoiding the individual-differences model altogether. In the presence of a structural explanation of stratification, the continued insistence that there must be individual differences begins to sound ideological.[9] What is more, the structural mode of explanation is the only one suitable in cases where we have decided for one or another a priori reason, that we want an explanatory frame which does not differentiate or discriminate among individuals. As we will see later on, there can be perfectly good methodological, even *ethical*, reasons for insisting on this. But for now, the primary justification for these structural explanations lies in their explanatory power and in their ability to show how much stratification is the result of system structure.

There is a certain objection which Marxists might make to this kind of explanation, for in a way, most Marxists agree with social Darwinists that individual differences explain why someone ends up in one class rather than another. They disagree (fundamentally) about what those differences are. They would cite a host of bad qualities to explain why someone becomes a capitalist: rapaciousness, greed, willingness to cheat or exploit others, willingness to enter the slave trade, and a host of other characteristics. And, on the historical question of the actual evolution of capitalism they would point out that the homogeneous

9. Especially when these differences are supposed to be the primary justification for the distribution of holdings.

market of Smith never existed. There were always asymmetries in economic power, they point out, and these became the basis for stratification in capitalism, together with a number of straightforward *acts* by the powerful to seize even more power: land grants, the Enclosure Acts, and the like.

This is true, yet I do not think it undercuts the explanation I have been urging, because focusing on those individual differences will lead to the incorrect conclusion that those differences cause stratification. The structural explanation has the virtue of being able to accept differentiating factors while correctly relegating them to their secondary role. And second, it is applicable in cases where those individual differences do not obtain.[10]

Human Nature: Biology and Philosophical Anthropology

Human nature explanations have a long history in social theory; there is hardly a phenomenon that someone has not tried to explain by appeal to human nature. Sometimes these natures are conceived philosophically: Hobbes's view of man's natural appetites and aversions, Hume's account of the passions, the "state of nature" conceptions of Locke and the social contractarians, Smith's *homo economicus*, and a long list of others. Another type of human nature explanation, not entirely distinct from this, finds the human essence in biological nature. This type of explanation has become very popular in certain circles, and we have seen attempts at biological explanations of war, aggression, social stratification, competitiveness, and sex-role differentiation.

The object of explanation in such cases is not, as in social Darwinism, individual differences. Here, what is being explained is a uniform characteristic of society. The basic structure of these biological explanations is that they seek to show that the given social phenomenon arises out of some trait inherent in the nature of the human individual. The overall social fact is seen as the product of collecting individuals each of whom has the individual trait. Social space is the product of N copies of an individual space, whose shape is given by individual nature.

10. For example, in the Soviet Union in the years immediately after the revolution, land reform was carried out by breaking up large estates into small, individually held plots with the usual structures of capitalist agriculture. Within ten years the size of land holdings had reverted to the prerevolutionary sort. There were a few large holdings and many who had been driven out altogether. It seems natural to try to explain this structurally.

The explanatory frame, then, is basically the same one that we confronted in the case of the ideal gas in thermodynamics: first an individual nature is postulated, and then the system properties are explained by aggregation. Let us review some of the problems of that example which are relevant here. The individual "nature" was that of tiny, Newtonian, elastic particles, and the aggregation of a number of such independent particles was supposed to produce the overall properties of the gas.

The problem was that the overall properties of the gas, like the Boyle-Charles law, did not arise simply from this individual nature; we had to make additional assumptions about the form of social organization of the molecules, assumptions that amounted to a nontrivial sociology. For example, we had to assume that the spacing among the particles was large enough that intermolecular forces played no role and also that certain kinds of energy exchanges took place. The individual nature produced the overall result *only* in a definite range of social forms.

The same thing is true in the case of society. We are told, for example, that people have an innate aggressiveness which is used to explain war. But surely the individual trait aggressiveness (whatever it is) does not produce war in every conceivable range of social environments; it must be somewhat sensitive to the range of environments in which it finds itself. We can imagine forms of social organization in which aggressiveness would not surface in war, say, by maintaining some kind of social spacing or by channeling the aggression somehow.

This dependence on social structure means that any attempt to explain a sociological trait by appeal to a biological trait will be at best elliptical. There is always a structural presupposition, so we can say once again that the explanatory frame is not

biology $\longrightarrow$ sociology

but rather

biology $\times$ sociology $\longrightarrow$ sociology.

The effect of suppressing the structural presuppositions is that the resulting statement gives us a false picture of the causalities involved. Consequently, many of these "human nature" explanations are like explaining the existence of restaurants by saying that people have to eat. We can grant that it is human nature that people have to eat, but, we want to ask, why should that necessitate *restaurants*? Think of all the specific content which is contained in the notion of a restaurant: a store selling prepared food for cash, to be served to the buyer and consumed on the premises. All that human nature requires is some way of getting food to people; hence that additional content in the notion of a restaurant is not necessitated by individual nature but rather by the need to satisfy that nature within a very definite context of social relations.

The general point here is that individual nature radically *underdetermines* the form of social organization, and hence the actual behavior, of the individuals. This point holds more widely than just in social systems. In many cases in the nonsocial sciences we also find that the laws which specify individual nature do not univocally determine the actual behaivor of the individuals but allow a number of different behaviors consistent with them.

For example, in the simple case of the solar system, simplified to the three-body problem of classical mechanics, the law of individual behavior is given by Newton's law of gravitational interaction. The actual, elliptical orbit of the earth is only one of several possible solutions to these "individual nature" equations. Other possible behavior forms include hyperbolic trajectories (like a comet) and even bizarre orbit shapes.

A similar statement can be made about one of the favorite examples of human nature theorists: competitiveness. Many have tried to explain the competitive features of society by postulating an innate tendency to selfish competition. Rousseau provides an interesting kind of objection to such explanations, very much in line with the underdetermination thesis. He distinguishes between two different notions: *amour-de-soi* (self-regard) and *amour-propre* (selfishness). He points out that self-regard is obviously deeper and more basic than selfishness and that if we assume human nature to include self-regard, then self-regard requires and becomes selfishness when placed in a competitive situation. We only have to make the weaker assumption of self-regard, and then we can explain selfishness nontrivially as the product of nature together with a specific form of social organization.[11]

11. Rousseau's explanation can be extended even further. The same self-regard which produces selfishness in one set of conditions can produce cooperative behavior in another. It should be fairly easy to model this kind of phase transition by using a game in which individual strategies are viable for some values of a crucial parameter, but where, as the parameter passes a critical point, coalitional strategies become optimal. Explanations of this kind are especially deep because

A similar underdetermination applies to the supposed biological basis of sex-role differentiation. One hears slogans like "anatomy is destiny," but this is absurd on the face of it. The fact that women are anatomically adapted to bear children in and of itself implies very little about the kinds of social roles they can or will fill. Considered in this light, it seems absurd to claim, as some popular writers do, that there is implicit in the anatomy of the womb a complete sociology of the nuclear, mommy-makes-dinner-and-daddy-comes-home-in-the-evening family. It is another case of the fallacy of telescoping the structural presuppositions into the biological premise.

The same lesson recurs in discussions of human nature in social theory, biology, political theory, or anywhere that this kind of argument flourishes. Scratch "natural man" and you find a complicated set of sociological assumptions. Each model of the pure individual turns out, on examination, to be more accurately a model of an individual in a definite set of social circumstances. A good example of this is Hobbes, whose *Leviathan* tried to derive a conception of society from a set of assumptions about natural man, a set of physiological properties concerning appetite and aversion. C. B. Macpherson's *Political Theory of Possessive Individualism* provides a good critique of this derivation:

> It is commonly said or assumed, by those who take the traditional view of Hobbes, that his psychological propositions are about man as such, man completely abstracted from society, and that those propositions contain all that is needed for his deduction of the necessity of the sovereign state.

But, he says, such an argument commits the fallacy of suppressed structure; Hobbes's natural man is in fact the child of extensive sociological assumptions:

> If by his psychological propositions we mean those propositions about sense, imagination, memory, reason, appetite and aversion, in which Hobbes describes the human being as a system of self-moving, self-guided

---

they show how the simpler theory arises as a limiting case of the more complex theory. Instead of assuming the behavior in question to be universal, they assume some more basic property and then show how the behavior in question arises in a certain range of boundary conditions. Such an explanation is deeper in two ways. First, it *explains* the behavior in question rather than simply *assuming* it. Second, it shows that the behavior is not necessary for all possible cases and shows what would have to be the case for it to be otherwise.

matter in motion, . . . then Hobbes' psychological propositions do not
contain all that is needed for the deduction of the necessity of the
sovereign state. If, on the other hand, we use the term psychological
propositions to include Hobbes' statement of the necessary behavior of
men towards each other in any society, then . . . they are not about the
human animal as such; some assumptions about men in civilized society
had to be added. . . . And the further assumptions are tenable only
about the relations prevailing between men in a certain kind of society. . . . Hobbes' state of nature or 'natural condition of mankind' is
not about 'natural' man as opposed to civilized man but it is about men
whose desires are specifically civilized.[12]

It is interesting to note that the move that I have been calling the
fallacy of suppressed structure has been offered by some as an explicit
foundation for methodology in social science. For example, it lies
behind the standard conception of so-called ideal types. Max Weber
introduced the term *ideal type* into social theory in his 1904 article,
"'Objectivity' in Social Science and Social Policy." He argues there that
the social scientist proceeds by abstracting from the concrete details
of actual social situations to arrive at an "ideal type" much like the
natural scientists' mass points and frictionless planes. In this early work,
these ideal types are of holistic or structural states of affairs: "mature
capitalism," "the democratic state," and so on.

But there is a significant shift in Weber's later writings: ideal types
become purely individualistic. J. W. N. Watkins cites this approvingly:

In the *Theory of Social and Economic Organization* ideal type construction means (not detecting and abstracting the over-all characteristics of
a whole situation and organizing these into a coherent scheme, but)
placing hypothetical, rational actors in some simplified situation, and
in deducing the consequences of their interaction.[13]

These individualistic ideal types are found throughout social theory.
In the standard expositions of the market, an ideal type is constructed,
a utility-maximizing rational entrepreneur, *homo economicus.* A collection of such individuals produces the usual economics. The same
method is used in rational preference models of political theory. First,
the individuals choose among social policies on the basis of self-

12. (Oxford: Clarendon Press, 1964), pp. 17–18.
13. J. W. N. Watkins, "Ideal Types and Historical Explanation," in A. Ryan,
ed., *The Philosophy of Social Explanation* (Oxford: Oxford University Press,
1973), p. 92.

interest. Then, an aggregate "social choice function" is constructed out of the individual preferences.[14]

In the example of the gas we said of the individual molecules what Macpherson said of Hobbes's natural men, that they contain structural presuppositions. In the case of the gas, one of the presuppositions is that the intermolecular spacing is sufficiently large that the other, non-mechanical forces do not come into play. If that social spacing were not the case, as in highly compressed gases, intermolecular forces of attraction would come into play, and the Boyle–Charles law would no longer hold. The defect of the pure individual in social theory is similar.

We can develop a style of criticism based on this observation which would apply to all sorts of individualistic constructions. The essence of the criticism consists in learning to ask, Can you find the structural presuppositions hidden in this picture?

In social choice theory each individual forms a preference schedule independently of everyone else, independently of what others might choose or desire. Moreover, the choice is made purely on the basis of the return to that individual. My returns are independent of anyone else's returns. We have already seen how this assumption distorts the model. It leaves out all the interesting questions: how those choices came to be related to one another, and how there came to be *those* choices at all. Those are issues which are taken as given.

When a model builds into the description of the ideal individual aspects which are really structural, it is dangerous to employ it as a tool in social policy. This is because it distorts the causalities involved and therefore gives a false picture of the possibilities for change. The tiny elastic particles model is successful in providing a reduction of the Boyle–Charles law. Impressed with the success of this reduction, we might think that we had really found the true nature of the gas molecules. This would be a mistake. The true nature of the molecules is really much more complicated because they have several different kinds of forces and bonds on one another, which operate only at short range. If we inferred from the successful reduction that the molecules really were

14. The classic sources are Kenneth Arrow, *Social Choice and Individual Values* (New Haven: Yale University Press, 1951); J. Buchanan and G. Tullock, *The Calculus of Consent* (Ann Arbor: University of Michigan Press, 1962); A. K. Sen, *Collective Choice and Social Welfare* (San Francisco: Holden-Day, 1970); and M. Olson, *The Logic of Collective Action* (Cambridge: Harvard University Press, 1965).

tiny, hard, elastic particles, we would end up concluding that it was impossible for such molecules to become a liquid; after all, the liquid state would violate individual nature!

We must be careful not to commit this fallacy. A construction of an individual nature, even if it is successful in explaining some of the features of a system, cannot be used as a basis for projecting what *other* modes the system may have, since, as in this case, a given model may explain one aspect of the behavior yet fail completely to explain other aspects.

The reductionist would, at this point, say something like this: Very well, the simpleminded atomistic model of the gas is mistaken. But a more complex one will work. If the gas is not a collection of tiny elastic particles, it *is* a collection of tiny elastic particles with little hooks, which are unhooked in the gaseous state and become hooked in the liquid state.

There are several problems with this reply. First of all, note that the new, improved theory of individual nature emerges only *after* we have observed the new mode or phase, and that this mode or phase was predicted impossible by the first theory. So we are in a somewhat odd situation: individual nature theory 1 predicts that the mode of social organization must be X. It turns out that this is false, that Y is a perfectly possible mode of organization. But Y is inconsistent with theory 1, so we move to theory 2, which accounts for the possibility of Y and so on. The individual nature theory is always one step behind the times.

Such false predictions will not cause great problems in the case of gases and other natural objects. We can see easily enough that water *is* capable of a liquid phase and hence can infer to the sort of individual nature that would at least make such a phase possible. In social theory this is not the case. The prediction that some overall phase is not possible, given individual nature, is *not* an invitation to falsify the claim by actually producing the phase, as it is with gases. The prediction of impossibility in the social case yields the imperative *not* to try to produce the phase. For if it is impossible, attempts to produce it will be frustrated and will produce unanticipated and unwanted consequences. The pain of adopting individual nature methodology in social theory is that at each phase-transition point, we would make the false prediction that the next form is impossible.

A second reason that this method is not advisable in social theory has to do with the extent to which individual behavior depends on social forms. In the case of the gas the number of overall modes is small: solid, liquid, gas, and a few other extremal or transitional phases. Moreover, the gross theory of overall changes is fairly simple and easy to describe empirically. We know what the control parameters are and how the overall state depends on them. We know that the crucial parameters are temperature and pressure, and that if we pass through certain critical values of them, we get a change of state. Yet, even though this theory is relatively simple, it should be pointed out that there is, at this point, no satisfactory individualistic theory which accounts for this. Few people are aware of this, and think: surely there must be a decent theory of the nature of the H_2O molecule, from which one can derive the theory of the various phases and their transitions. But this is not true. Such a theory simply does not exist, and attempts to formulate one have run into deep difficulties.[15]

But in the case of social systems the situation is even worse for the atomist. In the case of the gas there is at least some theory on the individual nature of the atoms; there is a theory of the chemical bond. But in the social case, even the kind of links which hold among the individuals is a function of the mode of social organization. A covalent bond is a covalent bond, in chalk or in cheese. But to say that two individuals are bound by the relation "husband-wife" or "landlord-tenant" is to say something which depends very heavily on the particular social structure in which it is found. What the nature of the relation is, and hence what sort of individual behaviors it allows, varies from structure to structure.

In other words the basic difference between the gas case and the social case is this: In the gas case it makes *sense* to talk about individual nature independently of the overall phase. (Although it makes sense, it is still fraught with difficulties.) In the social case, on the other hand, it does not even make sense. Human beings acquire in situ all their interesting capacities for behavior: language, rationality of various kinds, and so on. To be sure, the *possibility* of these things must be inherent in the nature of the individual. Individuals must have the perceptual apparatus necessary to discriminate others' speech, the brain capacity to store a vocabulary and rules of grammar, and so forth. But the kinds of basic relations which obtain, the analogues of the chemical bond, are themselves social, and their nature depends on the shape of the overall social structure. Relations like worker-employer, producer-consumer,

15. See p. 61 above.

and landholder-tenant all exist only in specific social forms and inherit their dynamics from those forms.

. . .

The purpose of the last two chapters has been to argue against in-dividualism as a method in social theory. The kinds of complaints I have been raising are factual or scientific. It does not explain this, it cannot answer that, it suppresses this, it confuses that. So far I have avoided any excursion into question of ethics and values.

This cannot be avoided indefinitely. Such questions are obviously present. But in order to assess the values at issue in the question of individualist vs. structuralist explanations, we first have to discuss how, in general, explanations reflect values.

5 The Ethics of Explanation

Value-free Social Science

It is commonly said that social science can and should be value free. In fact the idea of value freedom is often held to be synonymous with being objective and/or identified with the essence of the scientific spirit itself. We often hear the call for a "scientific" social science, and generally the view that lies behind it is that science is objective in that it is value free.

In philosophy, this view is associated with the logical positivism that dominated the philosophy of science in the first half of this century. But it is more common these days among working social scientists than among philosophers. In fact something of an anomaly now exists. Positivist doctrines are reaching the height of their popularity in certain areas of social science at the same time as their final rejection by philosophers of science.

The ideal of value freedom has several sources. Partly it stems from a desire to build social science on the model of natural science; the ideal is of value-free inquiry "just like in physics."

But let us leave aside the question of whether physics really is value free. Let us also leave aside the question of whether the natural and social sciences, in view of the difference in their subject matter, could possibly have the same methods. I want to examine the philosophical foundations of this claim to value neutrality, foundations which lie in some form or other of *empiricism.* If we were to press the question of how social science can possibly be value free, the usual answer would be some version of the empiricist view of science. We would be told that value-free objectivity is possible because theories can be tested, confirmed, and disconfirmed by means of objective *observations.* These theory-neutral and pure observations serve as the standards against which theories can be tested. Consequently, the argument runs, theories can be accepted or rejected purely on the basis of objective observation and formal logic, sanitized of the corruption of values.

This view is familiar enough. Even in this extreme form one can find explicit exponents, and in one or another modified form it commands a respectable audience in academic social science. This is in spite of the fact that the main development in the philosophy of science in the last twenty-five years has been the thoroughgoing refutation of just these empiricist doctrines. Unfortunately, very little of the philosophical writing has been absorbed or even noticed by the social scientists. The work of philosophers like Quine, Putnam, Hanson, and Toulmin is not well known outside professional philosophy. Kuhn's *Structure of Scientific Revolutions* has had a certain vogue but even that is not well understood. It is surprising how little social scientists know about the difficulties of the simple model of observation and the confirmation of theories. For example, the work of Putnam, Hanson, and Toulmin has helped to show that observation is inevitably theory laden, and Quine and Rudner have argued that the confirmation of theories necessarily involves values. Very little notice has been taken of these arguments.

My concern here, however, is not to argue these issues but rather to make a parallel argument in the theory of explanation. For there is another basic source for the idea of value-free social science, another empiricist doctrine, this one about the nature of causality and causal explanation.

Its essence lies in a certain way of looking at the relation between social science on the one hand and social policy on the other. The idea is that the "factual" aspects of the policy decision can be separated and distinguished from the "value-laden" aspects. In this view pure science comes packaged as causal statements which, by their nature as causal statements, are value free. The values are then added by the policymaker. If there are complaints about some *application* of the scientific statement, those complaints should be addressed to the policymaker or adviser, the one who made the practical decision, not the scientist.

This is, for example, the line taken by Hempel in *Aspects of Scientific Explanation*. In the chapter called "Science and Human Values" he says that science yields only instrumental judgments, that an action M is good or appropriate as a means to a goal G.

But to say this is tantamount to asserting either that, in the circumstances at hand, course of action M will definitely (or probably) lead to the attainment of G, or that failure to embark on course of action M will definitely (or probably) lead to the nonattainment of G. In other words, the instrumental value judgment asserts either that M is a (definitely or probably) sufficient means for attaining the end or goal G, or that it is a (definitely or probably) necessary means for attaining it. Thus, a relative, or instrumental, judgment of value can be reformulated as a statement which expresses a universal or probabilistic kind of means-end relationship, and which contains no term of moral discourse—such as 'good,' 'better,' 'ought to'—at all.[1]

The idea is clear enough. Science gives us only conditional statements of the form "If . . . , then. . . ." These statements are perfectly value free, and the only place that values enter into the picture is when a policymaker decides to detach an "if" in order to get a desired "then."

This view of the value neutrality of causal explanation is widely held; it is the conventional wisdom among social scientists, who often invoke the comparison to physics: "Physics tells us only that an atom bomb, for example, is *possible.* It doesn't tell us whether or not to build one. It simply reports the true statement that certain causal relations hold in the physical world." It is a view summarized by a famous dictum of Max Weber's (which Hempel cites approvingly): "Science is like a map; it can tell us how to get to a given place, but it cannot tell us where to go."

The basic claim is that a certain division of labor can be effected. The causal reasoning is done by the value-free scientist, and the value judgments are made by the policymaker. The syllogism representing the practical judgment can thus be analyzed into a purely factual means-end premise and a purely evaluative end. The examples of Hempel and others have as their general form:

A causes B	(science)
B is desirable	(value)
do A	(policy)

or

A causes B	(science)
B is undesirable	(value)
avoid A	(policy)

There is a great deal that can be said about when inferences of such

1. C. Hempel, *Aspects of Scientifc Explanation* (New York: Free Press, 1965), pp. 84–85.

forms are valid or invalid. I will not attempt to do a general study of such practical syllogisms. My purpose here is to ask whether this division of labor can really be effected and whether the fact that the scientist makes causal judgments means that the scientific premise is value free.

Suppose for a moment it is true that practical reasoning can be represented as the sum of a causal premise and an evaluative one. Does this mean that the maker of the causal premise is engaged in value-free activity? There is reason to think not. Look again at the quotation from Hempel; notice what he says at the very end, when he is asserting that the causal premise is value free: he says that certain *words*—"good," "ought," and so on—do not appear in the causal statement. The implication is that a statement in which those words do not appear does not have any values in it. This is false. Someone can do wrong by making statements in certain contexts which contain no moral words and are causal in form.

For example, if you know that Anne Frank is hiding in the attic, it is morally wrong to utter the statement, "If you look in the attic, you'll find Anne Frank" in the presence of Nazi search parties. It is absolutely no defense in such a case to object that you were merely making a causal and therefore value-neutral statement. Thus, even if a statement has no value words it does not mean that *making* the statement in a particular context is necessarily a value-free act.

Simple as it is, this point seems to be missed by many people. Positivist philosophers missed it because of their emphasis on syntax over pragmatics. But others miss the point for more self-serving reasons: scientists who want to forget about, or encourage other people to forget about, the social contexts in which their research is being applied. The division of labor argument was very popular, for example, during the Vietnam War, when certain scientists were criticized for doing war-related research. "Look," they would say, "all I'm doing is abstract research on the relative effectiveness of defoliants (or the stability of helicopter gunship platforms, or the structure of field communication among the Vietcong). If you have some objection to what the Army is doing, shouldn't you take it up with them directly?"

I think we can reject this argument on the principle that someone who knowingly supplies a bad cause with scientific know-how, like someone who supplies it with guns, does wrong in doing so. There will be clear cases for this principle in highly applied sciences, as in the examples above. The situation gets more and more difficult to evaluate as the application gets more remote and as the science itself gets more abstract. Actually, any fact may end up aiding some evil cause. So what are we to do?

It may seem natural to object that the values in cases like these still arise outside science itself and that the "pure inquiry" does not embody values. Consider the simple statement "A causes B." Is that statement, taken by itself, value free? I suggest that it is not.

Partial Causality

It has been noted at least since Mill that if we look at the causal explanations that actually occur in science and in practical life, we see that they are, in a sense, *incomplete*. Explanations typically will mention only one or two causal factors of an event, yet cite them as *the* cause. We say, for example, that the striking of a match caused it to light. But the striking of the match is only one of a set of factors all of which had to occur in order for the match to light. All those additional factors, like the presence of oxygen and the dryness of the match, are somehow relegated to the background or otherwise taken for granted.

What makes us choose one factor instead of another as "the" cause of an event? One answer is found in Collingwood's *Essay on Metaphysics*, where he points out that a number of systematic *pragmatic* principles function to select out "the" cause. The main one is that the factors we cite as the cause are those over which we have some practical control. We typically will cite a factor which "it is in our power to produce or prevent, and by producing or preventing which we can produce or prevent that whose cause it is said to be."[2]

> Thus, if my car fails to climb a steep hill, and I wonder why, I shall not consider my problem solved by a passer-by who tells me that the top of the hill is farther away from the earth's centre than its bottom, and consequently more power is needed to take a car uphill than to take her along the level. . . . But suppose an A.A. man comes along, opens the bonnet, holds up a loose high-tension lead, and says: "Look here, sir, you're running on three cylinders." My problem is now solved. I know the cause of the stoppage. . . . It has been correctly identified as the thing that I can put right, after which the car will go properly. If I had been a person who could flatten out hills by stamping on them the passer-by would have been right to call my attention to the hill

2. R. G. Collingwood, *An Essay on Metaphysics* (Oxford: Oxford University Press, 1940), p. 296.

as the cause of the stoppage; not because the hill was a hill but because I was able to flatten it out. (pp. 302–03)

So the element which is brought into the foreground as "the" cause is the element over which we have practical control, while the rest is relegated to a background which is taken for granted or presupposed. It follows that in other contexts, different practical situations may call for different factors to be selected as the cause of the same phenomenon.

Samuel Gorovitz, in an extension of Collingwood's discussion, talks about the example of the striking of the match and offers another sort of context, in which a nonstandard factor would be cited as the cause:

A match, having been pulled from the assembly line in a match factory, is struck in a supposedly evacuated chamber, the purpose being to test the hardness of the match head. But the chamber has not been properly sealed, and the match lights. . . . The cause can reasonably be said to be the presence of oxygen, and not the striking.[3]

Thus, we have two different causal models, which we could represent as

$$\text{striking} \xrightarrow{\text{[oxygen ...]}} \text{match lights}$$

and

$$\text{oxygen present} \xrightarrow{\text{[striking ...]}} \text{match lights.}$$

Collingwood also remarks on the dependence of cause on context and says, in effect, that when there are different handles on the phenomenon, we may have different explanations; he calls this "the relativity of causes":

For example, a car skids while cornering at a certain point, strikes the kerb, and turns turtle. From the car-driver's point of view the cause of the accident was cornering too fast, and the lesson is that one must drive more carefully. From the county-surveyor's point of view, the cause was a defect in the surface or camber of the road, and the lesson is that greater care must be taken to make roads skid-proof. From the motor-manufacturer's point of view the cause was defective design in the car, and the lesson is that one must place the centre of gravity lower. (p. 304)

3. S. Gorovitz, "Causal Judgements and Causal Explanations," *Journal of Philosophy* 62 (1965): 695.

The point is clear but there is something odd about his story. The characters in the auto accident would shame Sartre in their insistence on their own responsibility. Real people in auto accidents do not tend to be existential heroes. In fact the opposite is true. In a real accident the driver would jump out of the car and blame the auto manufacturer and/or the road builder. The road builder, of course, would reply: "You idiot. The roads are fine. It's the junk cars they're making today." Perhaps, in the absence of the manufacturer, they could agree that *given* the present state of the roads and *given* the driver's tendency to take corners fast, the cause of the accident was the poor design of the car. Of course the manufacturer will say, "What can you do? When people drive like that. . . ."

The relation between causality and practical control is more complicated than Collingwood and the others have imagined. In certain cases the principle "Select as the cause those things over which you have control" is replaced by "Minimize your own role in all this by selecting as the cause those things over which you do *not* have control" The standard accounts of causal selection do not acknowledge this inversion of practicality. But it is clear enough that it happens.

Sometimes, of course, the standard criterion is invoked, where the practical demands of the situation require an explanation in terms of certain variables. Suppose, for example, that you are hired by a team as a strategist. Your job is to explain to the team why it won or lost each game. If the team loses, you will not be doing your job if you say something like "We lost because they have that great halfback, who ran all over us, and scored three touchdowns." Here Collingwood is right. Your employers will say to you, "Don't tell us that. Tell us what we could have done, but failed to do, to stop him." The principle "Don't blame the other team; explain wins and losses in terms of team policy variables" is a sound principle for an in-house strategist. What the team's *publicist* says can be quite different since the purpose in that case might be to shift the focus away from the team's weaknesses.

And so, if a causal model separates the causal factors into foreground causes and background conditions, it is evident that the choice of a specific model may be motivated by a desire to locate responsibility in one place rather than another. But the important thing is this: Even if this desire is absent, it can still make sense to speak of a causal model as loaded or biased, *independently of anyone's motivations.* This enables us to avoid the question of the intentions of the scientist, for we can say that a causal model is loaded in and of itself. This is crucial for understanding the role of such models in situations where the motives of the scientists may be obscure or controversial. What I am suggesting is that motives are irrelevant to the assessment of the ideological "load" in a particular causal model. The value ladenness is a fact about the explanation not its proponents. It is value laden insofar as it insists, as a prescientific requirement, that change come from this sector rather than that.

This is how ideology becomes possible. A woman goes to a psychiatrist and says that she has been having fights with her husband. The psychiatrist says something like this: "You are having fights with your husband. Let us see what you are doing that contributes to these fights. There must be *something,* for after all, it takes two to have a fight. So we have to work on whatever it is that you're doing." Obviously, the burden of change has been placed on the woman, for the psychiatrist has written the causal model

$$\text{wife's actions} \xrightarrow{\text{[husband]}} \text{fights.}$$

Such a choice of framework, I want to say, stands in need of justification, and we have not so far been given one. Why has one causal factor been let off the hook? Sometimes, this will be justified by the statement that it is the woman, after all, who is the patient, not the husband, and one must work where one can; or it may be accompanied by fashionable admonitions to the woman to "take responsibility." But the end result is the same. Employing this framework amounts, in practice, to exempting the husband from responsibility.

Even at this very simple level we can find examples of this phenomenon at work in social science. Consider the case of the wage–price spiral. We are told that the cause of the rise in prices is a rise in wages. Writing this as

$$\text{wages rise} \xrightarrow{\text{[???]}} \text{prices rise,}$$

we may ask, What factors are being absolved from causal responsibility? Obviously, one of the factors being held constant is the rate of profit. If profits were allowed to fall, a rise in wages would not produce a rise in prices. When this is pointed out, the response will be some further reason why profits *ought not* to decrease. In other words the defense of a particular framework will be explicitly in ethical terms. Something like "profits are necessary for growth" will be suggested as the defense of this background condition, or perhaps "investors deserve profit as a reward for investing." I am not concerned here with the exact nature of such defenses or with actually evaluating them. I want only to point out that they are required. In the typical case such justifications are not offered or are offered only in response to objections. The student is simply told that a certain causal relation holds. The fact that such justifications are usually omitted is doubly significant, for the choice of framework amounts to a choice of who is to bear responsibility.

Consequently, if the "scientific" premise, the statement "A causes B" is a statement of partial causality and cites only some of the causal factors, the whole syllogism will suffer. In such a case, drawing the conclusion "avoid A" from the premises "A causes B" and "B is undesirable" is simply fallacious, as in the case of the psychiatrist above. (We could call the fallacy the *argumentum ad Valium*.) If the woman's conduct, A, is something like "wanting to take an evening class," then the result of the practical syllogism will be that this must be avoided. Obviously, this advice is heavily loaded and not at all value free.

So this is a clear case of what we had set out to look for: a situation in which the causal premise itself was not value free. We could try to eliminate this value ladenness by taking a certain way out. Because examples like these are generated by seizing on one factor and holding it up as *the* cause, it seems natural to think that when we have brought *all* the factors up into the foreground and suppressed nothing, we will have achieved the kind of causal explanation necessary for value-free social science.

The idea that we must eliminate partial causes is very common among writers on the subject. The tradition begins with Mill himself, who laments the tendency

> to give the name of cause to almost any one of the conditions of a phe-
> nomenon, or any portion of the whole number, arbitrarily selected. . . .
> It will probably be admitted without longer discussion, that no one of
> the conditions has more claim to that title than another, and that the
> real cause of the phenomenon is the assemblage of all its conditions.[4]

There is almost universal agreement that the way out of this unfortunate value-ladenness is to fill out the partial causal model to the full causal

4. J. S. Mill, *A System of Logic* (New York: Longmans, Green, 1936), bk. 3, chap. 5, sec. 3, p. 403.

explanation, in Mill's terms, "the sum total of the conditions . . . which, being realized, the consequent invariably follows."

This is the sort of explanation which the positivist writers, especially Hempel, cherished as the archetype of scientific explanation. The key feature is that, to rule out any partial causes, the thing cited as the cause must really be sufficient for the effect. In Hempel's model this sufficiency becomes complete logical sufficiency; the explanation logically entails the thing to be explained. Because of this it is not susceptible to the sort of fallacious usage that we saw in the case of the psychiatrist. If A really entails B, and B really is undesirable, then we really must avoid A. (Supposing, of course, that other conditions have been met. There may, for example, be means–end problems, or problems about balancing competing considerations.)

So it looks as if the way to avoid the hidden ethics lurking in the causal premise is to use the Hempelian model of explanation. The model presupposes that there is, in some statable form, the "full" cause of a given event. I suggest that there is no such thing and that there really is no way out of this ethics of explanation.

Are There Complete, Presuppositionless Explanations?

We are looking for an explanation which gives us the full cause and therefore is not subject to charges that it has arbitrarily (or worse) selected one causal factor. In order to see why such explanations are impossible, we must return to the earlier discussion of explanatory relativity, and ask: the full explanation *of what*? We might be tempted to say: of the event or state of affairs in question. But this is not so easy as it seems. Suppose the event in question is the auto accident I had yesterday. What is the full explanation of it? As we saw, if the object of explanation is that very accident, there is no such thing as the full explanation of it, for it would involve the whole history of the world, back through Henry Ford, the discovery of America, etc. If the object in question is a concrete particular, there is in some sense a "bad infinity" of causal factors.

Chapter 1 argued that to avoid this bad infinity, we had to introduce another piece of structure into the object of explanation: a sense of what will count as a relevant (or an irrelevant) difference from the event in question. Why this auto accident—rather than what? Rather than another ten feet down the road? Rather than no accident at all? Rather than one which was fatal? Each requires a different explanation.

Lacking this sense of what is to count as a relevant difference, there

is no single explanation "of E." In the typical cases in which it looks as
if we have a full explanation, we can find an implicit contrast space
and we will have the explanation of why E rather than the contrast.

The effect of these contrast spaces is similar in a way to the suppressed
causal antecedents. Both of them raise ethical problems.

Recall the Willie Sutton example. Sutton was asked why he robbed
banks and gave as an answer, "Well, that's where the money is." Sutton's
answer, I wanted to say, was really an answer to why he robs banks *as
against robbing some other kind of thing.* It does not explain why he robs
banks as against not robbing things, which was the priest's real question.
The contrast space builds into its structure what is to count as a relevant
alternative to the phenomenon, and the explanation explains E only as
against the limited alternatives in the contrast space. The consequence of
this is that once again certain possibilities are being excluded a priori
from consideration. This will stand in need of justification.

The way in which the contrast space can slant the analysis is already
obvious in the Willie Sutton case, and it is worth looking at its function
in more serious cases. Recall the discussion of explanations of unemployment; we discussed a number of examples in which the explanation
sought to explain unemployment by citing factors which differentiate
employed people from unemployed people, saying that S is unemployed
because S has property F. Now we said that such explanations do not,
in fact cannot, explain why there is unemployment at all. Rather, they
explain why, given that someone is to be unemployed, it is S instead
of someone else. To put it another way, all the elements in the contrast
space had some people being unemployed; they differed only as to whom.

When we use explanations like that in practical reasoning, it has the
obvious consequences. Because the existence of unemployed people is
common to every element in the contrast space, it is presupposed by
the explanation and therefore it is taken as unavoidable, practically
speaking. All advice generated by this contrast space takes for granted
that someone is to be unemployed; its problematic is limited to shifting around the names of the unemployed.

Such a constrast space allows us to ask only certain questions about unemployment and prevents us from asking others. As a consequence the
judicious choice of a contrast space, as in the Sutton case, has an effect
similar to the suppression of antecedents. Both limit the field of possibilities by what amount to prescientific requirements.

It will be clearer how such a limitation of possibility is value laden if we recall how explanations function in practical reasoning. Their role is to give us information on how we can produce or prevent the object in question. But then it follows that what exactly is taken to be a relevant alterantive to the object in question is going to have a profound effect on what sort of methods will be allowable ways of producing and preventing it. Recall, for example, the "preventing" syllogism. This syllogism enables us to go from the explanatory premise "A causes B" to the advice "To avoid B, avoid A." But if the object of explanation, B, is relativized to a definite range of alternatives, the allowable "negations" of B will be only a limited set. For example, suppose we construe the object of explanation in the Sutton case as why he robs banks rather than robbing some other thing and hence receive the explanation that banks have more money. Now if we plug that into the practical syllogism, we get the advice that, in order to prevent Sutton from robbing banks, we must make it be the case that something *else* has the most money, perhaps by placing large amounts of cash in grocery stores. But that is absurd.

The point is this: since an explanatory framework allows only certain alternatives to B, any advice which the theory generates will be advice only on navigating among its recognized alternatives. And so an explanatory framework can be value laden by having a truncated or deformed sense of possibility. This feature plays the same role as the suppression of antecedents in the case of the woman and the psychiatrist in requiring that change come from this factor rather than that.

This phenomenon is deeper than the value ladenness associated with the Collingwood–Gorovitz model and its suppressed antecedents. The way out of *that* relativity appeared to be the insistence on the *complete* antecedent. Whether or not there is such a thing and whatever it might look like if there is, such a move does not work against explanatory relativity. For, if I am right, we can speak only of the complete antecedent of B-relative-to-X, where X is some definite range of alternatives. The relativity to a contrast space (or more elaborate form of explanation space) is an additional dimension of relativity, distinct from the suppression of antecedents.

Nevertheless, one might be tempted to take a similar line in response to it. That is, one might try to derelativize the object of explanation: Why not try to get the full explanation of E as the explanation of why E-rather-than not E? Such an explanation would not be subject to explanatory relativity.

The problem is that there is no such full explanation. In order for a why question to be determinate, some nontrivial contrast space must be supplied. If E is the event being explained, then the "full" question Why E-rather-than-not-E? has as its answer the totality of history up to that point. As we saw, in order to get a manageable explanation we have to supply a contrast as an additional piece of structure. This means that there is an inescapable way in which explanations are value laden.

We saw how this makes for practical syllogisms which are "loaded" in the case of the negative mood ("A causes B" entailing "To avoid B, avoid A"). A similar situation is found in the positive mood, in which the causal premise "A causes B" generates "In order to get B, do A."

There are many reasons why inferences of this form might be invalid. For even if B is desirable, it does not follow that we ought to do A. It is, for example, silly to burn down the barn in order to roast the pig, even if we do want to have roast pork and even if burning the barn down really would cause that to happen. There may be problems about balancing the means against the end. But even leaving those aside, it still doesn't follow that we should do A to get B, for the simple reason that there may be some *better* way of getting B. For example, it might be worthwhile to walk all the way across town (A) in order to hear a concert (B), but it does not follow that we should do A, because there may be some A', which would also bring about B and which is better than A (say, taking a bus across town).

Consequently, if we are really going to generate an injunction to do A, we must in some sense be able to say that A is the best, the optimal, of all the potential causes of B. And here we face the problem that we have just appealed to the totality of *all* ways of getting B. But any explanation of B gives no such thing but only a small budget of ways of getting B-rather-than-something-else. Value consequences follow from the choice of what is to count as a relevant alternative to B.

Recall Weber's dictum: "Science is like a map, it can tell us how to get to a given place, but it cannot tell us where to go." We can now see how mistaken this is, first as a claim about maps and second as an analogous claim about science. Realize that any map gives us only a *handful* of ways of bringing about a given B (say, "getting to Philadelphia" or "heading north out of San Francisco"). The typical map gives us only major, paved, automobile roads as possible means to the end. Alternatives like striking out over land or burrowing through the earth, to say nothing of more serious possibilities like flying or taking a dirt road, are disqualified from consideration. The presuppositionless map, the map that would be truly value free, would have to make no such "arbitrary" choices. But that is clearly impossible. In a way unintended by the positivists, science really *is* like a map and displays the same selectivity and relativity to purposes that maps do.

Laws in Explanations and How They Are Value Laden

So far I have been talking about explanations in terms of their explanatory relativity structures. It might be useful, in addition, to talk about the ethics of explanation in a more familiar setting, the conception of explanation as proceeding via *laws*.

In the classical account of Hempel and Oppenheim an explanation is a deduction (C, L) → E, where E is a sentence describing the event to be explained, C is a statement of antecedent conditions, and L is a law.

But C and L, while they are both premises in the deduction of E, do not function equally in practical reasoning about E. The difference comes out when we seek to avoid or negate E. Ordinary logic tells us that, since C and L logically imply E, then, if E is to be false, either C or L must be. But in Hempel's account of the role of causal explanation in practical reasoning and in his (and others') example of it, this is not the case. The negation of E yields, not the expected "not-C or not-L," but simply "not-C." The practical syllogism does not recognize the possibility of the law's being false. Indeed, if it were possible that the law be false, it would not be a law.

In order to see the effect of this, we must look more closely at the notion of a law. Whatever else laws are, it is crucial that a real law be distinguishable from a mere accidental generalization which just happens to be true. All writers on the subject take pains to point out that although a law is a true statement of general form, say,

All F's are G's,

not every such statement, even if true, is a law; it might just be accidentally true. Thus, although

Everyone in this room is under 6′5″

may well be true, it is not a law. This is important because only a law can function as an explanation of anything. You cannot, for example, *explain* why I am under 6′5″ by deducing it from the statement above and the antecedent condition that I am in this room.

The difference between such accidental generalizations and real laws is that accidental generalizations do not give us any information about counterfactual possibilities. Real laws entail counterfactual statements. From the law "Sugar is soluble," we can derive the counterfactual statement that *if* this piece of sugar *were* to be placed in water, it *would* dissolve. No such thing is true of an accidental generalization; the corresponding counterfactual

> If anyone were to be in this room,
> he or she would be under 6'5"

is simply false.

All this is clear enough and can be found in any standard account. It is much less clear what counterfactuals are and how their truth is ascertained. This much at least seems to be true: a law must hold, not only in the circumstances which happen to obtain but also in a class of *possible* situations. There is a space of possible worlds in which the law retains its validity.

The difficulty arises when we try to say of *what* range of possible worlds the law must be true. Obviously it cannot be *all* possible worlds, for this would make the law into a logical truth and therefore vacuous. So the space is not just the actual world, and it is not all possible worlds; it is therefore some intermediate space.

Let us imagine a simple law of the form

> All F's are G's,

functioning in a simple explanation of why X is G, namely, that X is an F and all F's are G's. We can say that the law must retain its validity under certain perturbations of the actual situation; that is, it must retain its validity in some neighborhood of X in the space of possible worlds. If X was just a little bit different from what it actually is, the law should still apply to it. We can thus imagine a region in that space which is the domain of validity of the law; we can call this, with some justification, the *essence* of X. As long as the actual situation remains essentially the same (in this sense), the law, and hence the explanation, retains its force. The size and shape of the space, therefore, tell us how much is being presupposed about X.

Consider, for example, the case of explaining the final position of an object by appeal to an initial position and the law of falling bodies. The explanation therefore has the form:

X was in position F

All F's are G's

X is in position G.

Now consider the law: all F's are G's. Notice (as was pointed out on p. 39) that the relation between F-ness and G-ness does not hold for *all* things, only for physical objects. If X is a shadow, the law does not hold. So in this case the essence of X is that it is a physical object, for that is the region in which the law retains its validity.

Obviously, by taking a small space of possibilities as our intermediate or essence space, we can get an explanation which features a law valid only in that space. This method can be used to generate the "biased advice" cases we have been talking about. Recall, for example, the case of the woman and the psychiatrist. If we take as our space of possibilities only those situations in which the husband's behavior remains the same, we have a "law," valid in that space, according to which continued behavior of the same (innocent) kind by the woman will lead inexorably to fights. In general, what is wrong in such cases is that they feature too narrow a sense of possibility, hence too narrow a conception of the alternatives. This is especially significant in social theory, for there the laws are typically ones whose domain of validity is quite limited and whose projection across differences in time, place, culture, or social structure is at best hazardous. *Law's relativity*

Let us study an example to see how this works. Consider the economic law called the Phillips curve, which asserts that there is a fixed, ineliminable trade-off between unemployment and inflation: A low unemployment rate will cause a rise in the rate of inflation, and a high unemployment rate will cause a drop in inflation. This is the theory behind typical government economic policy.

Now I am not saying something controversial when I say that such a law is not valid for all possible social systems. For the primary mechanism which accounts for the Phillips effect is something like this: If unemployment is low, workers will feel bold about pressing wage demands because they do not fear the possibility of having to find another job. Moreover, low unemployment means that employers are bidding against one another in somewhat stiffer competition for labor, and so on. These factors make for higher wages. The transition from "higher wages" to "inflation" is effected silently, on the theory that employers will be forced to raise prices in order to meet these high wage

costs. Now whatever else we want to say about this law, it is clear that
this law is not valid in every possible economic system. There must,
for example, be a market in labor and a price system. If those things are
lacking, the Phillips effect does not hold. Thus it is trivially false in a
slave economy, where "full employment without inflation" is easily accomplished. Nor, on the other hand, does the effect hold in a socialist
economy.

Thus policy reasoning using the Phillips law will be reasoning under a
strong set of given constraints and will take the basic *structural* features
of the economic situation as given. Because those features are not really
fixed once and for all, *it will amount to a kind of value judgment to
act as if they are.* Suppose, for example, that someone carries out some
practical reasoning using the Phillips law and concludes that if inflation is to be lowered, unemployment must be raised. Then we could
reasonably ask, Why *must* unemployment be raised? Are there no
possible worlds in which we could have both low inflation and low unemployment? What gives you the right to suppose that the law is true
for every possible social world? The reply would be that of course the
law is not true in every possible social world; the person is not claiming that it is. Rather, what is being claimed is that it is valid in *this* world
and in the neighborhood of *practical* possibilities, "live" possibilities,
"realistic" possibilities. Such a person declines to accept certain possible
worlds as really possible and refuses to allow for their possibility in
practical reasoning.

The problem is that what is "realistic" to one may look myopic to
another. There may be genuine disagreement about whether an alternative economic system is "possible," not in the abstract sense of possibility, but in the practical sense: a possibility as something that must
be taken into account in practical reasoning. And so one person will
say that a certain alternative is possible and take it into account in practical reasoning, whereas another denies that it is practically possible.
What shall we say is the nature of the disagreement between two such
people? Is it a "factual" disagreement or a "value" disagreement?
There does not seem to be any clear separation between the two. The
question of whether something is possible has many of the features
of "factual" questions yet obviously has value consequences.

Sometimes these value consequences are denied, as when advocates of
a small possibility-space defend that choice as the purely personal decision to study one area rather than another. "Look," they will say,

"someone who chooses to study African history is not criticized for not studying European history. People get to choose what they want to study. The Phillips law is valid in a capitalist economy. We happen to live in a capitalist economy, and so the law is valid here and now. I choose to study the laws of capitalist economies, partly because that is the actual situation and partly because what I want to study is my free choice. If others wish to study the laws of socialist economies, let them do so; neither of us should be blamed for not doing the work of the other."

What is wrong with this response is that what we take to be ultimately possible has a significant effect on what we say about things here and now. The relation between unemployment and inflation, for example, is fixed only if we assume that the situation cannot go outside the boundaries of the capitalist economy; the economist who employs the Phillips curve is not just making the assumption that we are *now* in such a situation but rather that we will always, for the forseeable future, be in such a situation. This assumption about the future affects the kinds of causal statements and policy prescriptions that the scientist makes here and now.

For example, if we were willing to accept the possibility of the situation going beyond the confines of the market, unemployment could decline without prices rising. This would, however, entail the curtailment or outright suspension of the market. Perhaps it would be worth it. Perhaps it would not. My point here is only that this issue must be confronted, and one's choice defended. We cannot escape this requirement by pretending that the choice of framework is a harmless or "practical" decision.

In general, someone who sees some distant future state as a real possibility and takes that possibility into account in practical reasoning will end up acting differently from someone else who does not take that possibility seriously, or does not take it to be "really" or "practically" possible. One's horizons affect one's immediate actions.

Thus we see one way in which explanations come to have values. The choice of a larger or smaller contrast space makes for different applications to practical situations.

Individualistic versus Structural Explanations in Social Theory

Let us apply these observations about values in explanations to the controversy between individualistic and structural explanation in social theory. In the grading example of chapter 1 the teacher had decided in advance to grade on a curve, in fact, to give out exactly one A. It turned out that Mary was the person who got the A because she wrote the best final. We were able to distinguish two different questions that could be asked about this situation:

Q1. Why did exactly one person get an A?

and

Q2. Given that one person got an A, why was it *Mary*?

We called these, respectively, the structural question and the individualistic question. The important thing about these two questions is that the second one presupposes the first. The given clause of the second question amounts to presupposing that we have a satisfactory answer to the first. This presupposition can be seen on the logical or linguistic level as a relation between the questions themselves. But the linguistic presupposition also has practical consequences, for it turns out that what is linguistically presupposed is also practically presupposed. What is taken as given in the logic of the statements is also taken as given in practical reasoning.

The individualistic question takes the structural conditions as given. In particular it requires that we not question why the structural conditions are what they are but that we limit our questioning to states of affairs consistent with the structure. The consequence of this is that the individualistic question does not in any sense challenge the structure; rather, it chooses to accept the structure and sees its own problematic as navigating within it.

And so the individualistic framework ends up, in practice, supporting a proinstitutional bias. This is true in spite of (really because of) a tendency to view such questions as the practical question. There is a tendency to think of the individualistic problematic as the nonmoral or value-free approach, and this is how it is generally advertised. One hears things like: "We can't take up the question of whether the overall structure is fair or just. We have to be practical and avoid the ethical and philosophical problems. We must ask what can be done given the givens." This Thrasymachean outlook, of course, is not really the nonmoral approach it pretends to be.[5] The theory that accepts social

5. Cf. *Republic*, bk. I.

structure as given and seeks only to maneuver within it is not an alternative to moral theories; it is one among them. Socrates is right to argue that Thrasymachus is as much a moralist as he; they differ only in that Thrasymachus tries to disguise his moral choices as nonmoral "practicality."

But this practicality is purchased at the expense of committing the questioner to certain courses of action. This is especially clear if we look, for example, at individualistic explanations of unemployment. Here the nature of the individualistic problematic could be put as: Given unemployment, why is it this person rather than that who is unemployed? Someone operating within this problematic is seeking, in effect, to make sure that someone else gets unemployed. Each individual can adopt the advice generated by this framework and seek to get employed by having enough of the requisite individual predicates, but this advice cannot be simultaneously successfully followed by everyone. Each person follows the advice only by preventing someone else from following it. Hence there is a deep kind of inconsistency involved in saying to each person, Improve your individual properties.

Moreover, while people are running around trying to improve their individual predicates, the structural condition remains unaddressed. The effect of this is that the structure has received a silent blessing, accomplished by presupposing it and thus painting it out of the picture.

The result of this is to guarantee, automatically and by methodological fiat, that the "cause" of these problems is located in the individuals in a given situation, and not in the situation itself. This methodological shifting of responsibility can be carried out generally. If we are given an institution and a collection of people within it, we can take any effect of this interaction and ask what it is about the individuals (given the institution) that is responsible for the effect. This methodological bias constitutes the foundation of large areas of contemporary social science, especially social psychology.

Thus, if a group of children is failing in school, we can ask what about them causes this failure. Notice how natural that last sentence was, how easily the question suggests itself, and how hard it can be to see the proinstitutional bias that is built into it. The very use of the one-place predicate "failure," and others like "is violent," "is maladjusted," masks the fact that all of these are *relational* properties. It takes two to tango, and the "discovery" that there is something about the individuals in virtue of which they are at fault is not a discovery at all but a

decision to view the situation through the eyes of the institution. It
amounts to the decision to blame the individuals for the problems of
the interaction.

In extreme cases there is little else going on than these a priori requirements; the empirical part has actually shrunk to zero. After the so-called
riots in Detroit in 1967, Dr. Vernon Mark and Dr. William Sweet, writing in the *Journal of the American Medical Association,* had this to say:

> If slum conditions alone determined and initiated riots, why are the vast
> majority of slum dwellers able to resist the temptations of unrestrained
> violence? Is there something peculiar about the violent slum dweller that
> differentiates him from his peaceful neighbor? . . . We need intensive
> research and clinical studies of the individuals committing the violence.
> The goal of such studies would be to pinpoint, diagnose, and treat these
> people with low violence thresholds before they contribute to further
> tragedies.

The "treatment" they propose is psychosurgery: lobotomy and other
surgical techniques severing various connections in the brain and producing a passive (and therefore "nonviolent") subject. Given such a dras-
tic treatment, one would think that they would proceed with surgery
only where there is very hard evidence of specific brain damage or another, real, physiological condition, but this is not so. In fact the only
evidence that exists is the overt "antisocial" behavior. The inference
to an underlying physiological condition is purely a priori: there *must*
be something wrong with them because—look at how they're acting!
This move is an ethical disagreement disguised as a medical diagnosis,
together with a kind of mechanistic reductionism, in effect saying,
"After all, all behavior ultimately has a physiological basis, and so this
does too."

In fact their entire position consists of methodological artifacts. First
they set out a clear example of the individualist problematic:

1. There must be some difference between individuals who "riot"
   and those who do not.

Notice the *must:* the sure sign of a methodological requirement rather
than an empirical discovery.

The second key methodological move, after this individual difference
has been covertly postulated, is to announce that this difference, whatever it is, must be the *cause* of the violent behavior. In Collingwood's

terms it is the factor which we manipulate to bring about the desired effect. Here the desired effect is pacification.

Let us take the first point first. *Must* there be some difference between those who "riot" and those who do not? The answer, as we saw in chapter 4, is: not necessarily. There may be no significant difference between the individuals who engaged in violence and those who did not, just as there is no significant difference between the molecules which are precipitated out of a supersaturated solution and those which remain in solution. We can explain why X percent were precipitated without being able to explain, of those X percent, why it was *they*.

A similar situation seems to exist in ghetto rebellion. The significant question is, Why do large numbers of people engage in such actions? *not* Why *these* people rather than those?

In the second move, assuming that the individual differences are the *cause* of the violence and hence the element that is to change, they are committing the same fallacy we saw working in the case of the woman and the psychiatrist. Even if there *were* factors in those individuals which were part of the causal account of why they rebel, it does not follow that they ought to change, for they may be morally desirable! It may be, for example, that the people who rebelled (note the shift in terminology) had a greater capacity for moral outrage at the system or less passivity or fatalism. This view is ruled out of consideration by the problematic as the doctors frame it.

And so we see a striking, and tragic, example of how an individualistic problematic allows the scientist to blame the individual and absolve the institution. All this is achieved by choosing the right contrast space for the explanation. The same sort of thing will happen whenever (as, e.g., in educational psychology) the choice of explanatory frame amounts to a choice of who is to bear the burden of change and "adjustment." In these cases it is very important to see how these causal explanations are artifacts of the scientists' political and ethical values, prescientific requirements rather than scientific facts.

6 Beyond Relativism

Does Explanatory Relativity Imply Relativism?

Suppose there are values inherent in any explanation. Does this mean that all explanation is therefore subjective? That no explanation is better than any other? These are the questions I pursue in this chapter.

I have been arguing that there is an ethics of explanation. Choosing one explanatory frame over another has value presuppositions and value consequences. As a result of this the traditional conception of scientific objectivity as value freedom is untenable. This has been the thrust of recent philosophy of science.

Let us suppose that the positivist conception of mechanical, value-free objectivity is impossible. What are we going to put in its place? If the positivist model of scientific knowledge does not work, does it mean that there is something wrong with the model, or is there something wrong with the very idea of scientific objectivity itself?

Opinion is divided. Some think that the error lies in thinking that there is such a thing as objectivity at all. In this view the very idea of *truth* is the villain. The cure is a thorough-going relativism. Nothing is "true." You have your values and I have mine. From your perspective, X is "true," from mine, Y is, and nothing more can be said.

Such a view certainly rejects positivism but it also rejects a lot more: the notion of scientific knowledge itself. This kind of position has become much more popular recently among critics of science and amounts to an outright antiscientism or antirationalism.

The situation that has arisen is that the notion of scientific knowledge has become suspended between two extreme positions: the positivist conceptions of truth and objectivity vs. the antiscientific attacks on them. The truth, I think, lies with neither.

Consider, for example, the debate about whether scientific observation is objective. The positivists believed in a theory-neutral observation which would serve as the universal foundation for accepting and rejecting theories. The critique of this idea and the rejection of "immaculate perception" then lead to the opposite extreme, the view that all perception is subjective and personal and can validate nothing but the beliefs of the perceiver.

The same sort of opposition can be found in the controversy over how theories get corroborated. Some think that theory testing can be virtually mechanized, with formal procedures for telling us degrees of confirmation. Others think that theories are never really tested at all, that any evidence can be maintained in the light of any theory.

In the debate over the nature of explanation the positivist models explanation as formal deduction: a single, uniform model of a single, complete, correct explanation for a given phenomenon. Once we see how untenable that is and how much of a part values play in explanation, it can be tempting to go to the opposite, subjectivist extreme and deny that any explanation is better than any other. After all, what could make one better? From the point of view of one set of values, this and such may be the right explanation; from another set of values, something else may be right. You pays your money, and you takes your choice; nothing makes a given explanation objectively correct.

There is an important suppressed premise here, for the argument begins with the observation that explanations depend on values and proceeds to the conclusion that therefore there can be no fact of the matter about whether it is a good explanation. The suppressed premise is, obviously, that values are purely subjective, that there is nothing to say about whether one value is better than another. This seems to me to be mistaken. Explanations can be dependent on values without thereby becoming merely relative. For insofar as we can say that the values of one explanatory frame are more appropriate to the situation, or more just, or more conducive to human welfare than another, we can argue for the superiority of the relevant explanation.

Perhaps the simplest case of this sort is one in which the value preference is based on straightforward ethical considerations. Recall the example of the psychiatrist and the woman who was having fights with her husband. Suppose that the source of the fights was that she wanted to take a class one evening a week, and her husband insisted that she stay home to do household chores and respond to his requests for snacks. Now, from one point of view, the cause is the woman's insistence; from the other, the husband's refusal. But is that all there is to be said?

Some simple considerations can derelativize this situation. People have a right to certain kinds of self-expression and self-development; no husband has a right to demand that sort of subservience from his wife; no serious competing considerations have been advanced by the husband, only trivial ones. Considerations like these lead us to reject the husband's point of view and to hold the other explanation as the correct one.

Some will object that I am simply begging the question against *ethical* relativism. Perhaps I am. Perhaps it ought to be begged. We would need a major excursion into ethical theory for a general discussion of what is wrong with relativism. Fortunately, we do not need ethical theory to tell that the husband is wrong.

Of course, more complicated cases will not be so easy. There may be serious controversy about the superiority of one set of values to another and hence about what the right explanation is. If a man illegally carries a bomb on a railroad car and the bomb goes off, causing a heavy scale owned by the railroad to fall on Mrs. Palsgraf, is the railroad's scale part of the cause of Mrs. Palsgraf's injury? How we rule in this depends on whether we feel the railroad is responsible, in some ethical sense, for the injury. This can be debated. There may also be general policy considerations that suggest that the railroad should or should not be held responsible. One could argue, for example, that if railroads were to be held responsible, they would not be able to survive economically. Since it is in the public interest to have railroads, the railroad should not be held part of the cause. Here, what the correct explanation is can be a function of general theories of the public interest.[1]

A similar statement can be made about the ways in which explanations depend on purposes. We saw in the previous chapter that one explanation can work for one purpose and another for another. Sometimes purposes are equal and one has no claim over the other, as in the case of the home team versus the visitors. But are *all* purposes equal? Sometimes there are clear pragmatic reasons for preferring one purpose to another. In the discussion of reductionism in chapter 2 the argument was that there were certain important purposes for which reductionist (micro-) explanations could not serve equally well as the explanations they were supposed to be reducing. Recall the example of the foxes and rabbits. As an answer to the question Why did this rabbit die? there

---

1. H. L. A. Hart and A. M. Honoré's *Causation in the Law* (Oxford: Oxford University Press, 1959) contains an excellent analysis of these kinds of questions (see, e.g., their discussion of *Palsgraf* v. *Long Island R.R.*).

were two possible explanations, a microexplanation in terms of the positions and movements of the individual foxes and rabbits and a macroexplanation in terms of the fact that the fox population was high at that time.

These two explanations did not serve our purposes equally well. First, the microexplanation was completely unusable because of the staggering unwieldiness of an equation in thousands of variables, whose initial conditions must be known with impossibly great precision, and the computation of which would take years. No human being could ever employ such an explanation. Here, then, the purposes which make the one explanation superior to another are not specific or parochial ones but rather the general human purpose in seeking explanation itself.

Then there are other, more specific purposes which force a choice of one explanation over another. The microexplanation of the rabbit's death had as its real object the rabbit's being eaten by that particular fox at that particular time, and this is all the local equations can tell us. If we wanted to know what would have happened if things had been slightly different, the microequations are not much help, because they are hyperspecific. In particular, if we wanted to know what would have had to have been the case for the rabbit not to get eaten (by any fox), the microequations are useless. On the other hand the macroexplanation does give us an answer to that question.

So, if our purpose is avoiding the death of the rabbit and not just its death at the hands of a particular fox, we must choose the macro- over the microexplanation. But who is to say that this purpose is the decisive one? Well, *we* are. It is definitely more useful to be able to prevent the rabbit's death than to be able merely to prevent its death at a specific time and place.

Derelativizing Explanation

So there are at least two ways of arguing that one explanation is superior to another. It may proceed from values which are superior, or it may serve purposes which are more appropriate to our context. In this section I continue this line of argument by proposing additional criteria for deciding whether an explanation is a good one or is better than another. The previous section concerned ethical and purposive grounds for preferring explanations. But here my subject is simply what makes an explanation a *good* one.

My goal is twofold: first, to discuss general criteria for when one explanation is better than another, and second, to apply these criteria to the question of the relation between individualistic and structural explanation in social theory.

In the previous chapter the conflict between these two forms of explanation was left at a certain point. The individual and structural problematics were distinguished as being explanations in answer to different questions. I argued that those different questions had different value presuppositions and consequences. But the problem was left there: we did not have the right to say that one was *better* than the other, they were just—different. But I think that the structural explanation *is* in some sense better than the individualistic one, and this is what I will try to show here. I will apply the criteria for successful explanation to argue that in many cases the structural explanation is strictly better.

Let us begin with an observation about the foxes and rabbits. We noted in that case that the more detailed individualistic explanation of the death of the rabbit contained many factors irrelevant to that outcome. Therefore, the outcome would have occurred whether or not the antecedent of the explanation actually happened.

In the previous section this was presented as a fact about the unsuitability of the microexplanation for certain purposes. The general form of my complaint is this. Let us represent an explanation by the formula "P explains Q." Then if P contains many irrelevant factors, it follows that we cannot tell from this explanation what could cause Q *not* to be the case. In other words such an explanation does not tell us how to *avoid* or *change* Q.

The practical consequences of this are already clear in the foxes and rabbits case. The individualistic explanation gives us information sufficient to ensure that the rabbit gets eaten but says nothing about what might prevent the rabbit from being eaten. In particular, it certainly is not true that if the rabbit had not started out in this spot, etc., it would not have been eaten, for it is likely that the rabbit would have been eaten by some other fox. On the other hand the structural explanation, which explains the death of the rabbit by appeal to the high fox population, does tell us what would have to be otherwise for it to be likely that the rabbit not be eaten.

So the structural explanation tells us what the individualistic one does not: how to prevent the consequent. How important is this? Often, especially in social theory, the difference is crucial. In such cases we have a practical interest, like preventing or eradicating various social conditions (say, poverty or unemployment). But if the explanation is of the individualistic type, it offers us only a set of conditions which are mechanically sufficient to produce the outcome; we are not given precisely what we need.

There is an interesting lack of consistency in this regard in the writings of individualists like Karl Popper. One of the primary goals of his *The Open Society and Its Enemies* was to defend "methodological individualism" against "holism." Although these are methodological doctrines in the philosophy of science, Popper argues them largely on the grounds of the political consequences they have. Holists are totalitarians, he says, from Plato through Hegel and Marx, whereas individualists are liberals who believe in the "open society." The link between these methodological views and the political views they are supposed to represent is something like this. Holists believe that social change requires a change of the whole social system. Since such revolutionary change is obviously bad, says Popper, we can infer that holism is false (a very curious form of argument). The political approach associated with individualism Popper calls "piecemeal social engineering"; find a specific, concrete evil and work to eradicate it.

The paradox is that individualists in general, and Popper in particular, subscribe to a model of explanation which would make this impossible. For individualistic explanations are of the mechanical-sufficiency type, and such an explanation gives us no information on how to eradicate or prevent the effect. It would, of course, give us a *necessary* condition for avoiding the effect, in the sense that, if P is sufficient for Q, and Q is to be avoided, then P must be also. But we have absolutely no idea what to do in order to avoid Q, or which of the alternatives to P will work.

The reason why individualistic explanation does not work in these cases is that social systems typically have redundant causality. The redundancies in the ecological system ensure that the rabbit will be eaten in a large class of initial conditions, and this redundancy is typical of social systems. Remove a few individuals and the system remains essentially the same. Change the initial conditions or the nature of the individual dynamics over a wide range, and the overall system structure and dynamics remain the same.

Obviously, in cases which display high redundancy, explanations in terms of sufficient conditions will not tell us how to change their objects. This entails a serious objection to Popperian analyses of social systems.

We are supposed to engage in piecemeal social engineering, but the problem lies precisely in the impossibility, in typical cases, of proceeding piecemeal. The problem is that the phenomenon in question is connected in a redundant way with other phenomena. Therefore we have to know how the whole thing is wired up in order to see how to change Q. Otherwise, our attempts to change Q are likely to have untoward effects elsewhere or even to result in making Q be the case once again.

Attempts at piecemeal social engineering are notorious for this kind of problem. There is a problem, let us say, about traffic congestion on the old 2-lane road, so a 4-lane road is built. This piecemeal change works for a short time, but soon the attractiveness of the 4-lane road draws more people to use it, and soon we have heavy traffic on the new, wider, road. The reason for this is that there is a feedback mechanism operating, which the piecemeal approach could not take into account.

But the difference between explanations which provide counterfactual information and those which do not is important for more than "merely" practical reasons; in fact it is connected to the very idea of what a causal analysis is. We need a knowledge of how to prevent the effect, and hence need negative counterfactuals, in very basic kinds of scientific investigation.

We know, for example, that smoking causes lung cancer. Right now all we have is a causal explanation of the sufficient-conditions type: if someone smokes enough, the probability of lung cancer is much higher. But what we would really like to know is *what* about smoking causes cancer, that is, what it is in the cause that is crucial or essential to the production of the effect. We need a general account of the allowable variations in the effect. By means of something like Mill's methods, varying the causal factors one by one, we try to factor out the inessential until we have arrived at the kernel or the essence of the situation, that is, those things which are such that, had *they* not occurred, the effect would not have either.

I am saying, therefore, that there is something wrong with modeling the causal explanation as simply the giving of sufficient conditions. Moreover, what is wrong with it is not something which shows up only when we attempt to apply the explanation in practical affairs; it is wrong even as a model of pure scientific explanation. This is a defect of reductionist arguments, to be sure, but it even goes against the abstract Hempelian model of explanation itself, for the heart of that model is the fact that the antecedent constitutes a sufficient condition for the consequent.

There are two distinct strains in the history of analyses of causality, which can be roughly distinguished as focusing, respectively, on necessary conditions and on sufficient conditions. Interestingly, both take their modern origin from an assertion by Hume:

> We may define a cause to be an object, followed by another, and where all the objects similar to the first are followed by objects similar to the second. *Or in other words,* where if the first object had not been, the second never had existed.[2]

Now what can he possibly mean by "in other words"? Those two clauses have very little to do with each other and certainly do not say the same thing. The one speaks of sufficiency, the other of necessity.[3]

David Lewis notes this in a recent paper, remarking that "Hume defined causality twice over."[4] He observes that most modern writers have stuck with the first clause, sufficiency, and suggests a number of difficulties it faces: distinguishing causes from omnipresent effects, epiphenomena, and preempted potential causes. Claiming that "the prospects look dark" for a sufficiency analysis of causality, he offers instead an analysis based on necessity, that is, on the negative counterfactual. In such an analysis the explanation of the death of the rabbit in terms of such factors as initial positions turns out to be no explanation at all, since the counterfactual

> If the rabbit had not been at $x, t, \ldots$, he would not have been eaten

is simply false. In the corresponding causal claim, the antecedent is not necessary for the consequent.

2. D. Hume, *An Enquiry Concerning Human Understanding,* 2d. ed., ed. L. A. Selby-Bigge (Oxford: Oxford University Press, 1902), VII, ii (emphasis added).

3. G. H. von Wright, in *Explanation and Understanding* (Ithaca, New York: Cornell University Press, 1971), p. 184, notes this juxtaposition and calls it a "confusion." He cites Mill as subject to a similar confusion. I myself am confused as to how Hume and Mill could have been so confused. One is naturally reticent to attribute "howlers" to Hume and Mill, yet how are we going to make sense of what they say?

4. D. Lewis, "Causation," *Journal of Philosophy* 70 (1973): 556–67.

The Proper Object of Explanation

Our first complaint against the microobject in the foxes and rabbits case, that it did not lend itself to certain practical purposes, is connected to a more general claim about causal explanation per se. The source of the defect in the microobject is the fact that the system displays redundant causality.

In general, redundant causality makes for *levels of explanation*. Even if there is a microanalysis of the overall system, with each state of affairs assigned a microstate, the explanation of a given state will often be that the microsystem realizes a particular macrostructure.

Good examples of this phenomenon may be found in the attempts to explain social structures. Lévi-Strauss's *Elementary Structures of Kinship,*[5] to choose an example, is the classic study of *kinship structures:* ways of dividing societies into family groupings and relations, especially for the purposes of marriage. Kinship structures divide society into different classes, by means of which the eligibility of two people to marry each other may be determined. Given the class of an individual, the structure divides the rest of society into possible and forbidden spouses.

Anthropologists noticed that many kinship structures did what appears to us to be an odd thing: they distinguished between what are called cross-cousins, that is, between the daughter of mother's brother and the daughter of father's sister. We are likely to wonder what could possibly explain such a distinction.

In an appendix to Lévi-Strauss's book the mathematician André Weil proved a very interesting theorem:

> *Suppose* we have a kinship structure such that
>   (1) For each person, there is exactly one type that he or she can marry,
>   (2) For each person, the types of allowable marriage are determined solely by sex and the marriage type of the parents,
> *Then,* if the structure is to be arbitrarily perpetuable, a man will have either the daughter of his mother's brother permissible, or the daughter of his father's sister, *but not both.*

In other words, any system satisfying the assumptions which did not draw the cross-cousin distinction would find after time that there were

5. (Boston: Beacon Press, 1969).

individuals who could not be given a kinship status in a consistent fashion. So the distinction is necessitated by the requirement of stability over time.

Is this an *explanation?* I think it is, one of an interesting kind: an explanation of a structural fact (the cross-cousin distinction) by appeal to another structural fact (the requirement of stability over time). One property of a structure is explained by citing some other structural property.

Notice that if we look solely on the individual level we will miss this explanation altogether. The usual microreduction considers the actions of individuals to be basic. Thus J. W. N. Watkins says that we can reduce a social structure to "individual dispositions to maintain it." But where do these individual dispositions come from? How are they to be explained?

Of course we cannot explain these individual dispositions *as* dispositions to maintain the structure. The natives in the tribe do not know Weil's theorem, and they need not have any motivation, conscious or otherwise, to maintain the overall system. The structural explanation:

> stability → cross-cousin distinction

has no reality at the level of individual psychology.

What we *do* find on the individual level is individuals, acting for the sorts of local reasons that typically motivate individuals. If we look at the actions of person A, we find that *his* reason for drawing the distinction is that he was taught that it was important by person B. *Her* reason for thinking it important refers back to her relation with person C, who. . . . It is impossible, on this level, to see where this ends or when we have a genuine explanation.

Typically, explanations on the individualistic level display a certain circularity. We look at individual A doing X, and the microexplanation is that A is doing X because—everyone else is! This is often the only true explanation for why A is Xing. But then, of course, "everyone else" is just B and C and . . . , and for each one of them, we have a similar explanation: B is Xing because everyone else is, and so forth.

The circularity of the individualistic explanations makes them unsatisfactory. It does not help to be told that everyone is Xing because everyone else is. What we want to know is *not* "Why is everyone Xing?" taken one by one but rather in the sense of Why does this *practice* of Xing exist?

The answer to this structural question gives us an explanation of the overall practice and, importantly, tells us how to go about *changing* the practice. Notice that the strategy of changing the X-behavior of individuals one at a time is futile. For each individual the pressure of the others is sufficient to guarantee the Xing. On the other hand, if we have a structural explanation for the overall practice, we get an idea of how to go about changing everyone's behavior.

The phenomenon of each individual's behavior depending on everyone else's is found in all interesting cases of social practices. In economics, for example, the behavior of any single participant in an economic system must be explained in terms of what everyone else is doing. Yet this is unsatisfactory as an explanation. In the market, for example, each individual sets a price which is a function of the prices set by everyone else. Marx complains that if this is taken to be an *explanation* of prices, it is circular. (He calls it a tautology.) What he wants explained is why there is a given price system at all, and the individualistic level will not provide this.

The basic problem is that the phenomenon of interest *disappears* when the system is resolved into its individual components. This is not some mysterious fact about social systems but a very general property of levels of analysis in various kinds of complex systems.

Consider, for example, a vibrating string, whose resonance patterns we wish to study. The usual procedure is to assume that the string is a continuum and that its position is a continuous function of time.

In a sense this is false. Strings are not continua; in fact *there are no continua.* A string "is really" a very large number of molecules held together by binding forces of various kinds. The very idea of a physical continuum is, in a sense, a fiction.

But it is a useful fiction. For suppose we descend to the level of analysis of the string as a billion-body problem in particle mechanics. We get no better explanation of the gross properties of the string than we had before, and to the extent to which the billion-body problem *does* explain some property of the string, it is only because the billion bodies approximate a continuum!

Moreover, the continuous string, as a level of analysis, permits analytical techniques not available on the microlevel. For example, we can speak of the derivative of the string function and analyze various *causal* facts about the string as facts about the derivative of the function f. Such statements are obviously meaningful only on the macrolevel of analysis.

Considerations like these imply that some questions are only askable at a certain level of analysis. This, in turn, means that not all objects of explanation are created equal. Some give rise to relevant causal regularities and some do not.

This has been true in a number of the examples we have been reviewing. The overall form of these cases is as follows. First there is an individualistic level, a state space of huge dimension. By making various structural assumptions, we are able to reduce greatly the number of dimensions of the problem. In the case of the foxes and rabbits, for example, the problem can be reduced globally to a two-dimensional space (U = number of foxes, V = number of rabbits) with a global equation relating them. This equation says, in effect, that the only thing that is causally relevant to the (U, V)-level is the previous (U, V)-level. This, in turn, enables us to define an equivalence relation, "differs inessentially from": two microstates are equivalent if they have the same (U, V)-value. What is important in this case is that the equivalence relation is an equivalence from the point of view of causality: equivalent microstates have the same dynamical properties.

In such cases an explanatory advance is made by collapsing by means of this equivalence relation. If X is a given equivalence class [a set of microstates having the same (U, V)-value], we can answer the question that has the form Why X? without knowing *which* of the underlying microstates is in fact the case. Moreover, if we know the current *macrostate*, we can explain future developments of the macrostate. We can say that *some* member of the class Y will be realized. We cannot, at this level, say which member of Y it will be but then we do not want to. The idea is to forgo a certain specificity in order to get explanatory power, for it will be much easier to explain why *some* member of Y will be realized than it is to explain why, given that some member of Y must be realized, it is this one rather than that one.

Essentially the same phenomenon can be found in the other examples of the earlier chapters. The thermodynamics of gases, for example, illustrates a similar point. In that case the individualistic level consists of the locations and velocities of the individual gas molecules. Every molecule has a certain velocity, but the question

Why does m_0 have velocity v_0?

has no real nontrivial answer because the causal history which led to that state was a chaotic and unstable one. The slightest perturbation of of the initial state of m_0 would have resulted in a completely different history, at which we cannot even guess. When we pass to the statistical level of description, we forgo a great deal of specific explanatory power, the power to answer individualistic questions, but we gain another kind of explanatory power, the power to explain and predict certain *patterns* in the overall ensemble.

This becomes especially important in social cases, where in a similar fashion the choice of explanatory level affects whether we get a nontrivial explanation at all. We saw this in considering the analyses of economic distributions by Jencks et al. There the individualistic level consisted of questions like

Why does A_0 have economic status P_0?

and the answer Jencks proposed was: chaotic and random factors. We see now how this was produced by a focus on the wrong question. If we ask for the explanation, not of particular fortune and misfortune but of patterns of inequality, there *are* nontrivial explanations.

So the question is one of the proper object of explanation. The view I am suggesting denies the relativistic compromise of saying that one explanation is good for one object and another for another, because it holds that some objects are superior to others.

The general criterion relevant in the cases we are dealing with is that an object of explanation should be chosen which is *stable* under small perturbations of its conditions. In the whole microspace of the foxes and rabbits system there is a point corresponding to the death of that rabbit at the hands of that fox, at that place and time, and so forth. Now imagine a kind of mesh laid over the space, which determines what is to count as relevantly the same as that event. (This is, in effect, the contrast space of the explanation.) If the mesh is very fine, the resulting causal relations will be relatively unstable. Perturbing the initial conditions slightly will result in a situation which is different, inequivalent. If, however, we choose a mesh large enough (and cleverly enough) we can capture a stable relation, like the one between high fox populations and high likelihoods of rabbit deaths.

The weakness of the microreduction can then be put this way. Not only are the outcomes in the micromodel unstable under perturbations of the boundary conditions, but, what is worse, *the size of the perturbation necessary to destabilize the prediction is less than the degree of error introduced by the idealizing assumptions.* Real foxes will never correspond exactly to the ideal foxes of any model. But if the difference between foxes and ideal ones is large compared to the sensitivity of the model, the model becomes essentially and inherently useless.

Thus, all objects of explanation are not equal. Some give rise to stable causal relations or laws, and others do not.

Stability

The general criterion I am using, that a good explanation should be stable under perturbations of its assumptions, is worth discussing in its own right.

It occurs in an early form, and is explicitly defended, in an excellent account in Duhem's 1914 *The Aim and Structure of Physical Theory.* He says that a real fact is represented by a theoretical fact, which is therefore an approximation to it. The position of an object, for example, is represented by a mathematical point in a Euclidean space. But the real fact can be known only approximately; there is always some roughness in any measurement. Therefore, he says, the explanations we frame of the behavior of these quantities must be stable under small perturbations.

Suppose, for example, that we wanted to explain why a certain group of masses, the system of the Earth, the sun, and Jupiter behaved as they do. (This is the usual approximation to the solar system.) Suppose we are interested in why they have a trajectory of kind T. Suppose further that we could show that any three masses that had properties $P_1, \ldots, P_n$ would move in a T trajectory, and, lastly, suppose we have ascertained through observation that the Earth, the sun, and Jupiter actually have properties $P_1, \ldots, P_n$. It looks, then, as if we have an explanation of T, based on the deduction

$$\frac{\begin{array}{l} P_1, \ldots, P_n \\ (L){:}P_1, \ldots, P_n \to T \end{array}}{T} \; .$$

Yet this may fail as an explanation. Consider the law L. It *might* be the case that, while L carries the *point* $P_1, \ldots, P_n$ into a T trajectory, it is unstable at such a point and that points near $P_1, \ldots, P_n$ are carried into trajectories which do *not* have T. If this is the case, the above form is unsuitable for an explanation of T, because we cannot know that $P_1, \ldots, P_n$ are *exactly* correct, and if they are not, the explanation fails.

Duhem gives an example of this derived from Hadamard. A particle moves on a surface under some forces. There are some protuberances or horns on the surface. The possible world-lines or trajectories for the particle run all over the surface. Some wind around one horn, some wind around another, some wind around one horn for a number of turns and then depart for infinity.

We might try to employ this model to explain an actual trajectory, say, one that winds forever around one horn, by citing its initial condition and then proving that the trajectory through that initial position winds forever around that horn. But this would be fallacious as an explanation, Duhem says, if the law is not stable at that point. In the simple case studied by Hadamard, this actually happens: "The [trajectory] which remains at a finite distance while turning continually around the right horn will not be able to get rid of those unfaithful companions who, after turning like itself around the right horn, will go off indefinitely." (p. 141) This is true no matter how tightly we restrict the bundle of trajectories passing near the one in question. His conclusion is that

> a mathematical deduction is of no use to the physicist so long as it is
> limited to asserting that a given *rigorously* true proposition has for
> its consequence the *rigorous* accuracy of some such other proposition.
> To be useful to the physicist, it must still be proved that the second
> proposition remains *approximately* exact when the first is only *approx-
> imately* true.[6]

René Thom generalizes Duhem's criterion into an axiom for all mathematical models: since the real object is known only approximately, the model must be shown to be stable.[7]

It seems possible to give a general argument for such an axiom, an argument which is essentially Kantian: what are we justified in assuming in order that the situation be modeled at all? What must the objects of knowledge be like in order that knowledge of them be possible? In this case the problem is one of fitting idealized models to real objects.

Science, after all, deals in *idealizations*. We assume that there is no

---

6. P. Duhem, *The Aim and Structure of Physical Theory* (New York: Atheneum, 1977) (p. 143, emphasis original).

7. Cf. *Structural Stability and Morphogenesis.* Abraham's *Foundations of Mechanics* (1st ed.) contains an excellent discussion of the axiom of stability applied to models of the solar system.

air resistance or friction, that spheres are perfectly round, walls perfectly hard, collisions perfectly elastic. We assume that there are no transaction costs or that each player has perfect or total information. We assume that energy is conserved, that the diameters of the molecules are small, that intermolecular forces are negligible. We assume that the effects of any one trader on the market can be ignored, that the number of traders is large, or that the system is being viewed in the long run.

Of course, all of these are false. There is actually air resistance, spheres are never perfectly round, and so on. In the happy cases these idealizations *work*. That is, the fact that reality is not exactly as supposed by the ideal theory does not introduce any essential problems.

This is not always true. Sometimes the idealizing assumptions introduce fundamental error into the model. In such cases the theoretical results may be artifacts of the idealizing assumptions and hence inapplicable to the real world. In extreme cases, the idealizing assumptions make the model *completely* inapplicable to a given problem or produce paradoxical results.

Thus, we may study the collision of billiard balls by assuming that there is no friction. For certain purposes this idealization introduces no fundamental error. If the real world is tolerably close to the model, the collisions will be tolerably similar to the theoretical predictions. But for other purposes, for example, studying the long-run behavior, the idealizing assumptions render the problem incoherent. On a frictionless billiard table, all games last one shot.

Often, paradoxical conclusions can be drawn from the idealizing assumptions. We may assume that we are interested in the long-run behavior of the economic system, but, as Keynes observed, in the long run we are all dead. We may assume that space and time are infinitely divisible, yet this leads to Zeno's paradoxes. We assume in the ideal gas that the molecules have negligible diameters, yet this leads to Khinchin's paradox, described in chapter 2: infinitely small molecules must be bumping into one another with great regularity! We assume that a player assigns a utility to an outcome which is a real number, yet the probability of assigning any particular real number is zero.

The problem, then, is to be able to say when an idealizing assumption has introduced essential error for a particular application and when it has not. One condition clearly necessary for applicability is the requirement of stability in a certain characteristic form. Generally speaking, the idealizing assumption can be put in the form of an assumption that some parameter = 0. This may be the friction, the viscosity of a fluid, or the deviation from sphericality of a solid object. The question is then, Suppose the parameter is perturbed to a value ϵ, where ϵ is small but different from zero. What does the model look like then? If it is qualitatively different, our assumptions may lead to trouble. We can therefore say that one object of explanation is superior to another if it displays stability with respect to crucial perturbations.[8]

The Pragmatics of Explanation

One objection is likely to arise to discussion of explanations and purposes. It stems from a conviction that practical considerations should not be confused with logical ones and that purposes are really extraneous to a logical analysis of explanation. The positivist would say something like: "Your criteria for good explanations, being pragmatic, are not really part of the logic of explanation, but rather of its psychology or rhetoric. If, for example, a microexplanation exists in a particular case, reductionism is true. Whether you find such an explanation *convenient* for your purposes is another matter altogether."

This point of view is hard to justify in the case of explanations, which, as we have seen, are essentially pragmatic. The art of explanation *is* the art of throwing away almost all the data and forgetting almost all the conditions. How can we distinguish between what is necessary and what is (merely) convenient in the case of explanations, which are by their nature conveniences? The positivist wants to say that the explanations promised by microreduction are perfectly good ones, just inconvenient, since each one would be fatter than any telephone book. But explanations are functional things; they have a job to do and as such inherit the same "less is more" aesthetic that any functional object has. With such objects there can be no rigid distinction between something's doing its job badly and its simply not doing its job. If I offer you a carrot as a letter opener, is the carrot just a poor letter opener (one which is "inconvenient"), or do we want to say that it is no letter opener at all? There is not a sharp distinction to be drawn.

8. If the model does not display this stability for $V = 0$ we must go to a more complex model, in which $V = \epsilon \neq 0$ and which approximates the original model as $\epsilon \to 0$. Thus such cases are examples of a generalized correspondence principle, by analogy with the correspondence of special relativity to classical mechanics "at $V = 0$." The more complex theory is superior to the theory "at $V = 0$" because it contains the latter as a limiting case and shows the domain of validity and invalidity of the simpler model.

The positivist separation of logic and pragmatics meant that for many years pragmatics was the Cinderella of language, forced to stay home and do the dirty work while sisters syntax and semantics received all the attention. It was generally relegated to a mention in passing in the early pages of an author's work, usually consisting of the remark that pragmatic considerations such as friction and air resistance in mechanics would be ignored. This attitude was common to formal logicians like Carnap and Hempel, as well as natural linguists like Chomsky.

Wittgenstein and Austin led the criticism of this view, arguing that many of the crucial features of language, especially meaning and reference, could not be captured except by looking at the situations and contexts in which a particular piece of language functions and the uses to which it is put there. They emphasized language as an activity, as inherently functional.

The earlier, positivist, view had seen pragmatic considerations to be the sorts of things a scientific model would abstract from. In this new view they were the heart of the matter. "We have got on to slippery ice where there is no friction and so in a certain sense the conditions are ideal, but also, just because of that, we are unable to walk. We want to walk: so we need friction. Back to the rough ground."

My claim is that explanation is a similarly pragmatic notion. If what we want is a theory of explanation which accounts for when (and why) an explanation is not informative, not relevant, or beside the point, or begs the question, or is tautologous, or has the wrong presuppositions, or is useless to a certain purpose, or is not the sort of thing that could be an explanation, or does not have the right form, or asks the wrong question, then our theory will have to take into account the ways in which contexts affect the meaning of what is said.

For example, the discussion of contrast spaces and the relativity of explanation was a discussion from the point of view of the pragmatics of explanation. All the notions invoked there, like informativeness, speaking to the question, relevance, being "about" different things or the same thing, and utility in practice, are all pragmatic notions. A similar thing can be said about the requirement of stability. The idea that an explanation should remain "qualitatively" similar under "small" perturbations involves two pragmatic notions.[9]

9. *Pragmatic*, in this context, means that these notions are not simply functions of the meanings of the words involved but depend on the beliefs, purposes, and

I want to explore further one of the dimensions in which explanation is pragmatic: the way in which the object of explanation reflects what is, and what is not, being explained in a given case.

It is natural to want to say that an explanation is *about* the world. Explanations of the Civil War or of why the vase broke are in some sense *about* the Civil War and the vase. It also seems natural to try to explicate this concept of "aboutness" by the traditional notion of *reference*. The explanandum, the object of explanation, has a term which refers to a real object in the world.

But this real object is represented within the explanation as an ideal, theoretical object. Explanation is caught, and lives, in a tension between these two requirements. On the one hand, explanations are about the world and so must refer to real things. On the other hand, every explanation must have some generality, and so its object must in some sense be abstract.

In the simplest possible case the explanation concerns some concrete particular and explains why it has some property: why the vase broke or why these mice developed tumors. In such cases, as we have seen, the generality is expressed by the presuppositions, which reflect the domain in which the explanation is valid.

Serious difficulties occur as soon as we move away from this simple case to question the presuppositions themselves. Because the presuppositions reflect the domain of validity of a particular form of explanation, questioning the presuppositions amounts to asking why the form is valid, that is, asking why a particular pattern holds. Scientific activity consists essentially in activity of this kind. If mouse X develops a tumor, the question

Why did mouse X develop a tumor?

may be answered

because it was injected with agent Y.

But this answer wins no prizes. What we really want to know is a higher-order question:

---

so on of the speakers on a particular occasion. See R. Stalnaker, "Pragmatics," in D. Davidson and G. Harman, eds., *Semantics of Natural Language* (Dordrecht and Boston: D. Reidl, 1972), pp. 380–97, and S. Cavell, "Must We Mean What We Say?" in *Must We Mean What We Say?* (New York: Scribner's, 1969), for two different accounts of the pragmatic dimension.

Why do animals (mice? mammals?) injected
with agent Y develop tumors?

Scientific explanation questions the presuppositions of ordinary first-order explanation. We want to know why various *patterns* are the case: why people behave as they do, why ice contracts when heated, or why the levels of foxes and rabbits undergo oscillations.

The structure of the explanation of patterns is almost completely unknown. Hempel, for example, confesses that "the precise rational reconstruction of explanation as applied to general regularities presents peculiar problems for which we can offer no solution at present."[10]

I want to examine further the nature of such explanations, beginning with a linguistic difference between the explanation of patterns and the explanation of particulars.

Suppose someone asks the question

Why is Joan's husband a Democrat?

and receives the following two different answers to it:

Answer 1: "Because he's a liberal, you know, and liberals tend to vote Democratic."

Answer 2: "Why is her husband a Democrat? Oh, she's a lifelong Democrat herself. Her husband would have to be a Democrat; she'd never marry anyone who wasn't."

In answer 1, the speaker is construing the term "Joan's husband" to refer to a certain person and is explaining why *he* (however we refer to him) is a Democrat. In answer 2, on the other hand, the speaker takes as a live part of the explanation the fact that he is Joan's husband. In the first case there is substitutivity of co-referential terms, for the first explanation works equally well to explain why he, Harold, Sam's brother, and so on is a Democrat. But in answer 2 there is a failure of substitutivity. Explaining why Joan's husband is a Democrat in this sense does *not* also explain why Sam's brother is a Democrat, even though they are the same person.

The referring phrase "Joan's husband" is occurring in a different way in the two different cases. In the first case the function of the referring phrase is merely to mark the thing being discussed. The fact that the

10. *Aspects of Scientific Explanation*, p. 273.

thing being talked about (Joan's husband) actually has the property used to refer (being married to Joan) is not an issue for this explanation. In the second question, however, it is a live issue why the thing in question has that property.

The two different ways in which the referring term can occur is very close to a distinction drawn by Donnellan, who speaks of *referential* vs. *attributive* occurrence.[11] When a term occurs referentially, its function is only to pick out the subject of discourse, but when it occurs attributively, it is a live issue that the thing in question has the property. Although Donnellan does not treat the case of explanations, the structure seems close enough to warrant borrowing his terminology.

Questions in which referring terms occur attributively have a structure completely different from those in which the term occurs referentially. The fact that we cannot substitute one referring term for another which refers to the same thing is only the most obvious symptom of what is in fact a different kind of explanation.

For example, suppose someone asked in 1936, "Why is Roosevelt's running mate a southerner?" and received an answer, "In order to balance the ticket." The person giving the answer has construed the referring expression, "Roosevelt's running mate," to be occurring attributively. The symptom of this is the failure of substitutivity. Although

Roosevelt's running mate = John Nance Garner

it is false that the explanation explains why John Nance Garner was a southerner. (Indeed, it is hard to imagine what could possibly count as an answer to that question.)

What the attributive question is really asking can be put several different ways. We could say that the "the" that (implicitly) occurs in these referring phrases (the running mate of Roosevelt, the husband of Joan) is not the usual "the" but rather the *generic* "the" that occurs in phrases like "the whale feeds on plankton." This is a statement about whales, not about some particular whale, as "the whale was pursued by the Pequod" would be.

But appealing to the notion of the generic "the" is not really an analysis of the phenomenon. The crucial features of this kind of question are as follows. First, when someone asks why the X is G in this sense, they are

11. K. Donnellan, "Reference and Definite Descriptions," *Philosophical Review* 75 (1966): 281–304.

asking for an explanation of a general state of affairs: Why it is that *anything* which is the X must also be G. Second, they are asking why a certain causal connection holds: Why it is that anything which is the X *must be* G, not just why it happens to be G. What is really being asked is why a certain general causal connection holds between the property of being Joan's husband and the property of being a Democrat, or the property of being Roosevelt's running mate and the property of being a southerner.

Nothing in the traditional discussion of the logic of explanation equips us to handle this kind of case; it is a new variety of explanation, whose true nature is very different from its surface logic. The real nature of such questions cannot be brought out on the logical models because what they are asking is why a certain causal relation holds. In other words their object of explanation is

Why X causes Y.

This is not a well-formed object from the point of view of traditional logic. According to that viewpoint one should not explain why something causes something else; rather, one should explain why something happened by citing something which caused it. The notion of cause itself cannot appear among the things to be explained.[12] But that is just the point of the attributive question: to ask why a certain causal relation holds.

In fact we have been looking all along at examples of this type of question. The structural explanations that I have been defending are nothing more than answers to questions in the attributive sense. This distinction between these kinds of questions may help cast some light on the real difference between individualistic and structural explanation.

Structural Explanation

In individualistic explanation a question about a thing really is about *that* thing. We want to know why *Harry* is unemployed, why *Mary* got the A, and so on. As questions about those very individuals they take a standard form. A property of the individual is sought which differentiates that individual from the other individuals who do not have the trait

---

12. This is another legacy of empiricism, according to whch causality is not something *in* the world but only a mental judgment about the world.

being explained. The term which is used to refer to that individual is immaterial, that is to say, the term occurs referentially. If Mary happens to be the oldest person in the class, we can use that to refer to her and ask the question

Why did the oldest person in the class get the A?

If we really want to ask just the question why she got the A, the answer is

because she wrote the best final.

Notice that is what we want to know is why this person got the A, the referring term "the oldest person" must be construed to occur referentially.

If we read the occurrence in the attributive sense, we get a completely different question, for now the person is asking why a certain *connection* holds between being the oldest person and getting the A. In this reading, the answers are very different. If the question is

Why did the oldest person in the class get the A?

one possible answer is

Well, you know Aristotle says that ethics requires a certain level of maturity. Maybe being the oldest really helped her.

Or we might think that there really is no explanatory connection between being the oldest and getting the A. Then we would have to answer the question with something like

Why did the oldest person get the A? Gee, I don't know. No reason, really; it just happened that way.

Perhaps the most significant thing we can say about the structural question is that it amounts to questioning why the individualistic explanation *is* an explanation. Suppose the form of our question is

why the F is G.

If "the F" is occurring referentially, the answer will be some explanation citing a property of the F, including, possibly, the very fact that it *is* the F. It may be that the reason why the F is G is that it is, indeed, the F, and therefore, in that case, it would be nontrivial and explanatory to cite that as the answer to the question in this sense.

But suppose more generally that we have asked why the F is G, in the referential sense, and have received as an answer

because it is the X (and all X's are G's).

Here the person is saying that the fact that it is the X explains the fact that it is G. But suppose we could not accept this. Suppose we did not see *why* being the X explained the fact that it is G, or suppose that somehow we wanted to question the explanatory force of citing X as an explanation. Then the form that our further question would take would be

Yes, but *why* is the X G?

but this time with "the X" occurring *attributively*.

So the attributive question is the one which enables us to

(1) question the presuppositions of the individualistic explanation frame and
(2) ask why a general causal relation holds,

that is, the one which enables us to ask the structural question.

The various virtues which have been claimed for structural explanation flow from this characterization of it as involving such attributive questions. In particular this is true of what was said in chapter 2 about structural explanation being independent of the nature of the substrate. When we ask why the F is G in the referential sense, we are referring to the F, and asking something about *it*. But if we are asking why F is G in the attributive sense, we are not really referring to the thing which is the F; we are asking why anything which holds that position (of being the F) would be G, so our request is not about that thing and hence is independent of the particular nature of that thing.

In social theory the distinction between the two kinds of questions is most important, and here the interplay between them becomes even more complex. We can distinguish within social theory two different types of explanation. In one of them, which seeks to explain particular social states, the object of explanation is some identifiable individual's having some particular property, and the form of explanation is to cite a specific antecedent condition and a general law or rule. This was the case for Nozick's formulation of the market, in which the object of explanation is a set of actual holdings by identifiable individuals, and whose explanation took the form of an appeal to the laws of exchange and appropriation within the free market. It was also the case for social Darwinism, in which, again, the object of explanation was a set of specific people having specific social positions, and the explanation proceeded via the "laws" governing social mobility in the given system.

Of course, part of what is wrong with these explanations can be discovered only by looking at their *content*. One must look at exactly what the market advocates say about how markets operate, or what social Darwinists say about social mobility. But my point is that part of what is wrong with them can be grasped by an examination of their form alone; they are defective as explanations in the nature of their object and in what they count as an acceptable explanation of that object. This is so because, by their nature, they do not allow for the critique of laws and principles but rather take them to be given once and for all, with all explanation being explanation of particular configurations in terms of those laws and principles.

We need a form of social explanation in which social patterns and laws are the objects of explanation, not just the things which are the givens in explanation. This is, I said, the advantage of Rawls's approach over Nozick's; for Rawls the basic rules of society are to be explained.

Why do we need such a form of explanation? Why is it important for us to be able to explain social laws and patterns? Perhaps the most basic answer is that we want to be able to explain social laws because, ultimately, we can change them. The structuralistic point of view enables us to make social rules and institutions problematic in a way which the individualistic mode simply does not. This is especially valuable when we are looking practically at future social situations.

For example, several years ago the University of X announced that there would be a quota on tenure: only 60 percent of the faculty could be tenured. We were also told that, in light of this, some of the people we had nominated for tenure could not get it. And so the question arose: Which of the people nominated most deserved it? The dean turned to us and said, Well, which people should it be? Don't you want faculty control over something like that?

It became apparent that there was something wrong with this question, despite the fact that the question itself makes sense. The question

> Given that some people will be denied tenure,
> why should it be *those* people?

is a perfectly reasonable question. There *are* differences among people, and if only some could get tenure there were reasons why some of them would have more of a claim to it than others.

Nevertheless, despite the meaningfulness of this question, it had to be rejected instead of answered. What was wrong with it was that it had a presupposition, a given clause, that we were not prepared to accept as given, at any rate, at least not yet. We could not see why only 60 percent of the faculty should be tenured and, practically speaking, we did not accept this as a given. We intended to challenge it and had at least *some* confidence in our ability to affect the outcome, and so we saw the structural condition as problematic.[13]

But in order to succeed in our organizing against the tenure quota, we had to set aside any sort of inquiry into the divisive question of *who* should get tenure if we failed. In order to build a coalition that could actually have an effect on the 60/40 rule, questions of individual differences had to be ruled out of order as counterproductive.

For it is clear what would happen if those questions were opened. One person would say, "Well, certainly, if only some people can get tenure, this woman from History surely deserves it." And then someone from English would say, "Oh yeah? What about the Barzino thing? You didn't vote for that then, when it was our candidate. No, I think Ralph should get it. He's overdue."

And what can you say? He *is* overdue. But you think other considerations are more important. And what about the Barzino case anyway?

While we are thinking about this, we are doing nothing about challenging the basic presupposition of this entire line of inquiry. And it is not just that these questions take up time and energy that could be used for a better purpose, that they are a mere distraction like a television program; rather, the pursuit of that question would causally undermine the coalition which was needed. Consequently, by our very act of engaging in that line of questioning, we would have causally contributed to its presupposition's being true.

We were able to resist doing this, refused to rank our candidates, and instead organized against the tenure quota. As it turned out, more than 60 percent got tenure. The moral of this story is that there is a certain amount of existentiality to these situations. We are presented with a given, a *putative* given, and then we get to decide whether to

---

13. The belief in our ability to change the situation was necessary assumption, necessary for our activities to make sense.

accept that as given and therefore to reason within it. On the one hand, nothing *forces* us to take it as given. Even if it looks unavoidable, there is always *some* chance that if we committed ourselves totally to making the presupposition false, we could succeed. As a result some ethical responsibility is always incurred in accepting any situation as given.[14] But, on the other hand, if the situation really is not going to be changed, we ought to accept the structural condition and do the best we can within it. After all, suppose we had been wrong about our chances of getting rid of the tenure quota; suppose we had failed. Then some people would have been chosen without faculty input and with at least some risk that the wrong people would have received it. There are obviously cases in which it is wrong to try to challenge the presupposition, where the only right thing to do is to accept the given and work within it.

Cases like the tenure-quota case give us a new kind of situation in which the individualistic problematic is to be rejected. We saw cases where the question of individual differences was unanswerable for scientific reasons, cases where the individual differences were too small, too obscure, or too hard to ascertain historically for the question to be answered. But in this case the reason for rejecting the individualistic problematic is really ethical or strategic. We decided that the question of individual differences was divisive and therefore not a productive line of inquiry. The curious fact, and one that needs philosophical explication, is that by our decision not to accept the individualistic problematic, we were able to prove that it had a false presupposition.

This is true in all sorts of individualist problematics. One is never sure that the given clauses are really given ineluctably, and a decision to accept it means that *we* have guaranteed that it will be true. This is especially true in cases of scarce resources problematics. The general

14. Merleau-Ponty's *Humanism and Terror* contains a good example of this situation. The collaborators with Nazism said after the war, in effect: "Look, it was overwhelmingly likely that the Nazis would win. Faced with this fact, we resolved to make the best of this bad situation." Merleau-Ponty's answer is interesting. He says, roughly, that the Resistance had the same information and the same judgments of objective probability. But they resolved that however small the chance was, they would stake their future on it, and would not accept it as given. He therefore rejects the idea that the virtue of the Resistance lies in the fact that they were better trendspotters than the collaborators, that they just had a better reading of the future probabilities. And so we have a curious situation in which someone is morally blamed for acting on a proposition which was in fact highly probable.

form of such cases is as follows. A group of people is told that a certain fixed quantity X of some desirable good is available. The quantity X will be divided among the group, and so individual interests are in conflict. The more of X one member gets, the less there is for the others. The group is then invited to find some method of dividing the scarce resource.

It is natural, in such cases, to see the situation as essentially competitive. The very idea of scarce resources seems to imply that individual interests are in conflict. The only question seems to be: Who is going to get how much of X?

But the very fact that X is all there is, is itself problematic. After all, who is to say that this is true? We are told that the only question is the question of dividing X, but there is a prior question. If the group did *not* see itself as in internal competition for the scarce resource, would it be able to cooperate and thereby get *more* than X?

This point is fundamental for understanding the basic Marxist account of classes and class unity. In Adam Smith's presentation of the market it is a set of independent, homogeneous entrepreneurs, each trading out of self-interest. But it is not really homogeneous, for there are two different kinds of traders: those who own capital and are seeking to buy labor power, and those who are selling labor power because they have no capital of their own. The great advantage for the buyer of labor is that he is dealing with a number of people who are potentially in competition for jobs. Consequently, he can say things such as: I am offering X number of jobs at Y wages. Now *if* everyone accepts this, they *are* in competition and have thereby guaranteed that there will not be a higher wage. After all, why should the employer pay more when competition among the employees makes it unnecessary?

But suppose, on the other hand, that they organize a *coalitional strategy*. Then they can collectively hold out for a higher wage. This is the theory behind trade unions. I mention it here not in order to display Marx as the first game theorist, developing a strategic outlook for certain players in the job market game, but because it does provide an interesting set of examples of how complex the relations are among ethics, strategy, and modes of explanation.

For in order to organize the trade union, individuals have to renounce egoism, that is, to renounce egoistic claims against one another. Individual differences are rejected as being of no account.

This does not quite amount to an ethical rejection of egoism. For one

thing, the ultimate purpose behind forming the coalition is the further-
ing of the individual interests of the members. Each member rejects
any conception of an individual good that is not simp y an outcome of
the overall group utility. But the purpose of this *is* to further the good
of the individuals; if it did not have this effect, people would not do
it. On the other hand we cannot simply reduce the group good to the
sum of the individual goods and make the trade-union ethic simply a
sophisticated form of egoism, because there is not a quite perfect fit between the group utility and the individual utilities. Generally, whatever
serves the group serves the individuals too. But occasionally the coalitional strategy may force a hardship on someone. That person's self-
interest would *not* be served by the coalitional strategy, but the person
would be asked to go along with the coalition anyway. (The coalition
could try to show its good faith by making some compensation to such
people.)

It also does not amount to an ethical rejection of egoism because,
well, it is not really *ethical*. I do not mean that it is *un*ethical. It would
be better to see it as strategic. The injunction to reject individual
differences and to work for the collective good is not being argued for
on the basis of traditional ethical considerations. Rather, it is a principle of strategy.

Ultimately, considerations of this kind may be the most important
kind of argument for structural explanation in social theory.

Index